READING WORLD WITH FOLKTALES

By
Nancy Polette

Illustrated by
Paul Dillon

Pieces of Learning

1998 published by
Pieces of Learning

CLC0212
ISBN 1-880505-60-6

Printed in the United States of America

ACKNOWLEDGEMENTS

With the permission of the publishers, jacket copy is quoted in booktalks for *Ma'ii and Cousin Toad* by Shanto Begay, Scholastic Hardcover, 1992; *The Tale of Aladdin and the Wonderful Lamp* by Eric A. Kimmel, Holiday House, 1992; *Kiviok's Magic Journey* by James Houston, Atheneum, 1973; *Tattercoats* edited by Joseph Jacobs, illustrated by Margot Tomes, Putnams, 1989; *Lon Po Po: A Red Riding Hood Story* from China by Ed Young, Philomel, 1989; *Snow White and Rose Red* by Jakob and Wilhelm Grimm, Philomel Books, 1992; *The Surprising Things Maui Did* by Jay Williams, Four Winds Press, 1979; *The Old Woman and the Red Pumpkin* by Betsy Bang, Macmillan, 1975; *Chancay and the Secret of Fire: A Peruvian Folktale* by Donald Charles, Putnams, 1992.

Reading the World With Folktales
CONTENTS

1 United States Ma'ii and Cousin Toad
2 Arctic Kiviok's Magic Journey
3 Canada Ghost Horse of the Mounties
4 Ireland Finn M'Coul
5 Germany Snow White and Rose Red
6 France Puss in Boots
7 Norway Maid on the Glass Mountain
8 British Isles Tattercoats
9 Russia Salt
10 Italy Bell of Atri
11 Japan Tongue Cut Sparrow
12 China Lon Po Po
13 Australia Wombat Stew
14 India The Old Woman and the Red Pumpkin
15 Saudi Arabia Aladdin and the Wonderful Lamp
16 Nigeria Why Flies Buzz
17 Peru Chancay and the Secret of Fire
18 Mexico Gonyo and the Princess
19 United States: Hawaii The Surprising Things Maui Did

Reading the World With Folktales
by Nancy Polette

Introduction

As advances in communication and transportation have made the world smaller and smaller, it is essential that children today explore global education as an important component in the social studies program. And what better way to learn about countries of the world and their people than through the literature of each country.

Reading the World With Folktales introduces nineteen different countries by presenting a folktale readers theatre booktalk on each country. After performing the booktalk, students are given information about each country and are introduced to both creative writing and research activities centered around the country.

By using the literature, students should gain a greater understanding and appreciation of a variety of world cultures and at the same time realize that the problems of mankind are universal regardless of time or place and that we as humankind on this planet Earth are far more alike than we are different.

Reading the World With Folktales will allow students to walk briefly in the shoes of others they may never meet and to experience their hopes and dreams, their problems and successes, and to learn more about countries and cultures throughout the world.

Ma'ii and Cousin Horned Toad

A Traditional Navajo Story

Written and illustrated by Shonto Begay.

Scholastic Hardcover, 1992

Booktalk

American Indian

Up on the mountainside where the air smells like cedar and pine, tricky Ma'ii the coyote, is hungry. He decides it is time to visit his cousin Horned Toad, as he knows his cousin will feed him well. After all, Ma'ii likes a full stomach, not a noisy one.

Meanwhile, the diligent, hard-working Horned Toad is tending the cornfield when Ma'ii comes rudely crashing through. Nice fellow that he is, Horned Toad generously shares food with Ma'ii. But Ma'ii wants more. And he doesn't want to work for it. Perhaps, he thinks, if he swallows his small cousin, Horned Toad's farm will be his. But life is never as easy as one would wish, and from the belly of the cunning coyote, Horned Toad teaches Ma'ii that there's no such thing as a free lunch!

About the Author/Illustrator

Shonto Begay, one of sixteen children born to a Navajo medicine man, grew up in a hogan (built by his father) in Shonto, Arizona. "There as far as the eye could see," says Mr. Begay, "was the world that harbored the ancient gods and animal beings that are still so alive today in the myths of my people."

Shonto Begay studied fine arts in New Mexico and California and received a BFA with distinction. He currently lives in Keyenta, Arizona with his wife and three children.

About the Navajo Indians

The Navajos were a nomadic tribe that settled in the Southwest. Their traditional home was the hogan and some still live in hogans today. They farm, raise sheep, and many own oil, timber, gas and uranium sites. Many are skilled artists and craftsmen making colorful rugs, silver jewelry paintings and murals.

Ma'ii and Cousin Horned Toad

Performing the Booktalk

Speaking Parts: Narrator One, Narrator Two, Ma'ii, Horned Toad

Narrator One:	Up on the mountainside
Narrator Two:	where the air smells like cedar and pine,
Narrator One:	tricky Ma'ii, the coyote,
Ma'ii:	is hungry.
Narrator One:	He decides
Ma'ii:	it is time to visit
Narrator Two:	his cousin Horned Toad
Narrator One:	as he knows his cousin will feed him well. After all, Ma'ii
Ma'ii:	likes a full stomach, not a noisy one.
Narrator Two:	Meanwhile, the diligent, hard-working Horned Toad
Toad:	is tending the cornfield
Narrator One:	when Ma'ii
Ma'ii:	comes rudely crashing through.
Narrator Two:	Nice fellow that he is, Horned Toad
Toad:	generously shares food with Ma'ii.
Narrator One:	But Ma'ii
Ma'ii:	wants more.
Narrator One:	And he doesn't
Ma'ii:	want to work for it. Perhaps,
Narrator One:	he thinks if he swallows his small cousin, Horned Toad's farm will be his.
Narrator Two:	But life is never as easy as one would wish, and from the belly of the cunning coyote, Horned Toad
Toad:	teaches Ma'ii that there's no such thing as a free lunch!

Ma'ii and Cousin Horned Toad

Time for Skills! Making Words

Directions: Write each of these letters on a separate small piece of paper.

A C D E F L N O O R T

Use the letters to make words that will answer these questions.

1. What did Ma'ii want at the beginning of the story? Choose four letters to make the word.

   — — — —

2. Who had what Ma'ii wanted? Take away two letters and add two letters to make the word.

   — — — —

3. Toad wiped away the sweat to keep — — — — .
   Take away three letters and add three letters to make the word.

4. What did Toad give Ma'ii to eat? Take away two letters and add two letters to make the word.

   — — — —

5. When Ma'ii fainted from fright, Toad saw that he was out

   — — — — . Take away two letters and add two letters to make the word.

6. By the end of the story, Ma'ii decided to leave Toad

   — — — — — . Take away two letters and add three letters to make the word.

Answers: 1. food 2. Toad 3. cool 4. corn 5. cold 6. alone

Comparing Tales

The Dog and His Shadow
(from Aesop's Fables)

A dog spied a piece of meat hanging outside a butcher shop. Quick as a wink he grabbed the meat and ran off with it. Before long he came to a bridge, looked down in the water and saw his shadow. The dog thought that the shadow was a bigger dog with a bigger piece of meat. He jumped off the bridge to grab the other dog's meat. When he opened his jaws, the meat he was carrying dropped to the bottom of the river and the dog swam to shore with no meat at all.

Directions:
Work in small groups to discuss the question below. Each group should have a secretary to write the main ideas that are given. Be prepared to share your ideas with the rest of the class.

Question:

How many ways are the Aesop's Fable of the *Dog and his Shadow* and the tale of *Ma'ii and Cousin Horned Toad* alike?

Learning About Desert Creatures

Choose one of these desert creatures and find information about it.

rattlesnake	lizard	Gila monster
horned toad	coyote	kangaroo rat

Use the "Important Pattern" that follows to write about the creature you chose.

EXAMPLE: Coyote

The important thing about a coyote is that it howls at the moon. It is about the size of a dog, has a bushy tail and ears that stand straight up. It has soft yellowish fur and can run fast enough to catch a jack rabbit. It is sometimes called the Prairie Wolf. But the important thing about a coyote is that it howls at the moon.

YOUR TURN: Topic ____________________

The important thing about a ____________________ is that

____.

It ____

and ____.

It ____

and ____.

But the important thing about a ____________________ is

that it ____.

More Picture Story Books from the North American Indian

PICTURE BOOKS

Baylor, Byrd. *Moon Song.* Illustrated by Ronald Himler. Scribner's, 1982.
The moon deserts her son Coyote who howls for her each night.

Carey, Valerie Scho. *Quail Song: A Pueblo Indian Tale.* Illustrated by Ivan Barnett. Putnam's, 1990.
A traditional tale in which Quail outwits a persistent coyote.

Cohen, Caron Lee. *The Mud Pony.* Illustrated by Shonto Begay. Scholastic, 1990.
An Indian boy achieves greatness with the guidance of a pony he has made out of mud.

Esbensen, Barbara Juster. *Ladder to the Sky: How the Gift of Healing Came to the Ojibway Nation.* Illustrated by Helen K. Davie. Little Brown, 1989.
The legend of how Ojibway medicine men acquired their healing powers.

Esbensen, Barbara Juster. *The Star Maiden: An Ojibway Tale.* Illustrated by Helen K. Davie. Little Brown, 1988.
The legend of how water lilies came to be.

Goble, Paul. *The Gift of the Sacred Dog.* Illustrated by the author. Bradbury Press, 1980.
A myth telling how the Plains Indians got horses.

Goble, Paul. *Iktomi and the Buffalo Skull: A Plains Indian Story.* Illustrated by the author. Orchard Books, 1991.
Iktomi finds that trying to impress the Indian maidens results in much hardship.

Mayo, Gretchen. *Star Tales: North American Indian Stories About the Stars.* Illustrated by the author. Walker & Co., 1987.
American Indian legends about the moon, stars and night.

San Souci, Robert D. *The Legend of Scarface: A Blackfeet Indian Tale.* Illustrated by the author. Doubleday, 1978.
A young brave must travel to the sun to win the hand of his future wife.

NON-FICTION - INDIANS

Baylor, Byrd. *When the Clay Sings.* Illustrated by Tom Bahti. Scribner's, 1972. (Gr. 2-4)
A tribute to the prehistoric Indian in the desert West.

Osinski, Alice. *The Navajo.* Children's Press, 1987. (Gr. 2-4)
Traditional customs and changes brought by modern civilization.

NON-FICTION - DESERTS

Bender, Lionel. *Desert.* Watts, 1989. (Gr. 3-5)
How deserts are formed with information about desert animals and plants.

Catchpole, Clive. *Deserts.* Illustrated by Brian McIntyre. Dial Books for Young Readers, 1984. (Gr. 2-4)
Climate, plant and animal life of the desert.

The Tale of Aladdin and the Wonderful Lamp: A Story from the Arabian Nights

Retold by Eric A. Kimmel. Illustrated by Ju-Hong Chen.

Holiday House, 1992

Booktalk

Arabia

Long ago, in a distant city on the borders of China, there lived a clever but lazy boy named Aladdin. One day, a strange magician appeared, claiming to be the boy's uncle. He asked Aladdin to retrieve an old lamp from a dark, mysterious underground cavern. Aladdin completed the task, but when his uncle asked him for the lamp, Aladdin refused to give it up. Furious, his uncle trapped him in the darkness. Aladdin's luck changed, however, when he discovered that both the lamp and a magic ring, when rubbed, each conjured up a djinn or genie. With the djinn at his service, Aladdin's every wish came true. But the powers of magic are fickle, and when the magician returned to steal Aladdin's wife and castle, Aladdin had to find a way to put everything to rights again in the *Tale of Aladdin and the Wonderful Lamp.*

About the Author and Illustrator

Eric Kimmel has written, retold or adapted a number of stories from around the world. He is a Professor of Education at Portland State University and a frequent storyteller in schools.

Ju-Hong Chen was born in Shanghai, China, where he worked as a designer and artist from 1962 until he moved to America in 1982. He has illustrated a number of books including *The Fourth Question* and *The Jade Stone.* He lives in Portland, Oregon with his wife and daughter.

Pre-Reading Journals

One method which has proven effective in giving students a purpose and focus for reading is the pre-reading journal. Using this method, students respond to provocative questions dealing with plot or theme of a particular story, chapter or novel before reading the selection. After writing for about five minutes, students are encouraged to share what they have written orally. This is an ideal way to pull from the experiences of older students in preparing to read.

Advantages of pre-reading journals

Since journals are not graded for spelling, punctuation, etc., students can write freely about topics, discovering what they think or how they feel about the topic.

The lively discussion which follows is fueled by the free-writing experiences and prepares students for the selection to be read.

The daily writing activity and subsequent discussion helps students to become better readers as student interest in a topic is generated and students focus on concepts and ideas which will be presented in the reading.

For reluctant readers, the free writing time is a non-threatening way to prepare students for what they will be reading.

When students are allowed to concentrate on what to write rather than how to write it, higher quality responses often occur, reading becomes more relevant and students become better readers.

Sample open ended sentence starters for the pre-reading journal experience:

Aladdin and the Wonderful Lamp

1. Trickery can lead to disaster when...........
2. Being all alone in a dark cave...............
3. Riches do not always mean happiness, for example..........
4. If you had a magic lamp that would produce a genie.......

The Tale of Aladdin and the Wonderful Lamp: A Story from the Arabian Nights.

Retold by Eric A. Kimmel. Illustrated by Ju-Hong Chen

Performing the Booktalk

Speaking Parts: Narrator One, Narrator Two, Aladdin, Magician

Narrator One:	Long ago, in a distant city on the borders of China, there lived a clever but lazy boy
Aladdin:	named Aladdin.
Narrator Two:	One day, a strange magician appeared,
Magician:	claiming to be the boy's uncle.
Narrator Two:	He asked Aladdin
Magician:	to retrieve an old lamp from a dark, mysterious underground cavern.
Narrator One:	Aladdin
Aladdin:	completed the task,
Narrator Two:	but when his uncle asked him
Magician:	for the lamp,
Narrator One:	Aladdin refused
Aladdin:	to give it up.
Narrator Two:	Furious, his uncle
Magician:	trapped him in the darkness.
Narrator One:	Aladdin's luck changed however, when he
Aladdin:	discovered that both the lamp and a magic ring when rubbed,
Narrator One:	each conjured up a djinn or genie. With the djinn at his service, Aladdin's
Aladdin:	every wish came true.

Performing the Booktalk (continued)

Narrator Two:	But the powers of magic are fickle, and when the magician
Magician:	returned to steal Aladdin's wife and castle,
Narrator One:	Aladdin had to find a way
Aladdin:	to put everything to rights again
All:	in the tale of *Aladdin and the Wonderful Lamp.*

Responding To The Booktalk

In small groups, discuss this question:

> How many ways can you list that the tale of *Aladdin and the Wonderful Lamp* is like the tale of *Jack and the Beanstalk?*

Each group should have a recorder to list the main ideas that are given.

Be ready to share your group's ideas with the class.

Writing About Aladdin
The Important Pattern

Choose one of the following:

Aladdin lamp genie
underground cavern

Follow the pattern below to write about it.

The Important Thing About the Uncle

1. Make an important statement — The important thing about the uncle was that he was a magician.
2. Make three more statements about the topic. — He pretended to be related to Aladdin. He left Aladdin in an underground cavern. He stole Aladdin's wife and lamp.
3. Repeat the first statement. — But the important thing about the uncle was, he was a magician.

YOUR TURN

Topic ______________

The important thing about ________________________ was

____ .

1. ____

2. ____

3. ____

But the important thing about ____________________ was

____ .

More Books Tales From Arabia and the Middle East

PICTURE BOOKS

Accardo, Anthony (Illustrator) *Aladdin and the Wonderful Lamp and Other Tales of Adventure*. Golden Books, 1987.
Colorful illustrations highlight an anthology of favorite tales.

Carrick, Carol. *Aladdin and His Wonderful Lamp*. Illustrated by Donald Carrick. Scholastic , 1990. (Gr. 2-4)
A poor tailor's son becomes a wealthy prince with the aid of a magic lamp.

Gorog, Judith. *Winning Scheherazade*. Atheneum, 1991.
A retelling of the story with a desert adventure for Scheherazade.

Lang, Andrew. *Aladdin and the Wonderful Lamp*. Illustrated by Errol Le Cain. Viking, 1981.

McVitty, Walter. *Ali Baba and the Forty Thieves*. Illustrated by Margaret Early. Abrams, 1990.
Ali Baba's life is saved by the servant Morgaina after dangerous adventures.

Wolkstein, Diane (Reteller). *The Red Lion: A Tale of Ancient Persia*. Illustrated by Ed Young. Crowell, 1977.
Azgid must prove his courage by battling the red lion before be can become king of his country.

NON-FICTION - ARABS

Al Hoad, Abdul Latif. *We Live in Saudi Arabia*. Bookwright Press, 1987. (Gr. 4-6) Saudi Arabians from children to adults speak about their lives.

Dutton, Roderic. *An Arab Family*. Photographs by John B. Free. Lerner Publications, 1985. (Gr. 3-5)
The changes in the life of a farm family living on the coast of Oman.

Jacobson, Peter Otto. *A Family in the Persian Gulf*. Bookwright Press, 1985. (Gr. 2-4)
The home, work and day-to-day activities of a family in Bahrain.

Lye, Keith. *Take a Trip to Saudi Arabia*. Watts, 1984. (Gr. 1-3)
Describes the desert location, school and living standards of the people.

McCarthy, Kevin. *Saudi Arabia: A Desert Kingdom*. Dillon, 1986. (Gr. 4-6)
The people, geography, history, language and industry of Saudi Arabia.

Saudi Arabia in Pictures. Prepared by the Geography Department of Lerner Publications, 1988. (Gr. 4-6)
Introduces the geography, history, economy, culture and people.

Kiviok's Magic Journey

Written and illustrated by James Houston.

A Margaret K. McElderry Book. Atheneum, 1973

Booktalk

Arctic Regions

Kiviok is an Innuit folk hero about whom many wonderful tales are told throughout the Northwest Territories of Canada as well as Alaska and Greenland. It is said that he first appeared soon after the sun and the moon came to light the world.

In this tale he takes as a wife a beautiful girl whose white feather coat was snatched up by a wicked raven one day while she bathed in the lake with her sisters. The sisters, quickly pulling on downy coats, turned back into snow geese and soared into the sky, but Kungo was left behind. For seven years, she and Kiviok and their two children lived joyfully together, until the wicked raven came again and spirited Kungo and the children away.

Join Kiviok on his long and dangerous journey to search for his lost family...a journey that takes him far to the South and across a mighty ocean, there to confront the raven in a life or death struggle.

About the Author/Illustrator

James Houston was born and grew up in Ontario, Canada. In 1948 he made his first trip to the Canadian Arctic and discovered the remarkable art of the people in stone, bone and ivory carvings. He lived on Baffin Island in the Northwest Territories for twelve years, for nine of them serving as the first Civil Administrator of West Baffin Island. In 1972 he was appointed Officer of the Order of Canada.

Kiviok's Magic Journey

Performing the Booktalk

Speaking Parts: Narrator One, Narrator Two, Kiviok, Wife(Kungo), Raven, Sisters

Narrator One:	Kiviok is an Innuit folk hero about whom many wonderful tales are told
Narrator Two:	throughout the Northwest Territories of Canada as well as Alaska and Greenland.
Narrator One:	It is said that he first appeared
Kiviok:	soon after the sun and moon came to light the world.
Narrator Two:	In this tale he
Kiviok:	takes as a wife a beautiful girl
Raven:	whose white feather coat was snatched up
Kiviok:	by a wicked raven one day while she
Wife:	bathed in the lake
Kiviok:	with her sisters.
Narrator Two:	The sisters
Sisters:	quickly pulling on downy coats, turned back into snow geese and soared into the sky,
Narrator One:	but Kungo
Wife:	was left behind.
Narrator One:	For seven years she and Kiviok and their two children
Kiviok/Wife:	lived joyfully together,
Narrator Two:	until the wicked raven

Performing the Booktalk (continued)

Raven:	came again and spirited Kungo and the children away.
Narrator One:	Join Kiviok on his
Kiviok:	long and dangerous journey to search for
Narrator Two:	his lost family...
Narrator One:	A journey that takes him
Kiviok:	far to the South and across a mighty ocean, there to confront the raven
All:	in a life or death struggle.

Responding To The Booktalk

Work in groups of three or four to answer this question:

How many ways are *The Tale of Rapunzel* and *Kiviok's Magic Journey* alike? Can you find five? eight? ten? One person in your group can be the secretary to write the group's main ideas.

1. ______________________________
2. ______________________________
3. ______________________________
4. ______________________________
5. ______________________________
6. ______________________________
7. ______________________________
8. ______________________________
9. ______________________________
10. ______________________________

Write Your Own Legend About...

Legend

Here is an account of one incident in the life of ________________ ________________ . It is not clear whether this incident actually occurred, but knowing what history tells us about the life and adventures of ________________________________, it could possibly be true.

It happened ________________________ ________________________
when where

________________________________ that ________________
name

was ____

____

____

____

____

____ .

The reaction of the folks around was ________________________

____

____

____

____

____ .

Kiviok's Magic Journey
An Igloo Song

In the story Kiviok and his family lived in a tent in the summertime and in an igloo in the wintertime. Look at the information in the data bank about igloos. Use the information to write a song about igloos.

Data Bank - Igloo

Made Of
2' x 2' snow blocks

Shaped Like
dome
spiral
smaller at the top
10 feet wide

Has
a dome
small top hole
tunnel entrance
ice window
sleeping shelf

Where Found
Northern Canada
Alaska
Greenland

Song Pattern (Sing to the tune of "London Bridge")

An igloo's made of blocks of snow
Blocks of snow
Blocks of snow
An igloo's made of blocks of snow
With a tunnel entrance.

An igloo has ______________________

____

____

An igloo has ______________________

And is ______________________

More Picture Books About Northern Arctic Regions

PICTURE BOOKS

Andrews, Jan. *The Very Last First Time.* Illustrated by Ian Wallace. Atheneum, 1986.
A tale of the Innuit people who live along the seashore.

Beim, Lorraine. *The Little Igloo.* Illustrated by Howard Simon. Harcourt, 1941.
A dog can be important to an Arctic family.

Bonsall, Crosby. *What Spot?* Illustrated by the author. HarperCollins, 1963.
A walrus and a puffin in the frozen Arctic puzzle over a strange spot.

Damjan, Mischa. *Atuk.* Illustrated by Gian Casty. Pantheon Books, 1960.
The bravery of a dog and the danger of wolves to the Arctic family.

DeArmond, Dale. *The Seal Oil Lamp.* Illustrated by the author. Little Brown, 1988.
An Arctic tale of how a seven-year-old blind boy is saved from death by the mouse people.

Harlow, Joan Hiatt. *Shadow Bear.* Illustrated by Jim Arnosky. Doubleday, 1981.
A polar bear can strike fear in anyone who comes upon it.

Machetanz, Sara. *A Puppy Named Gia.* Illustrated by Fred Machetanz. Scribner's, 1975.
How important a dog is to a young Innuit boy!

Parish, Peggy. *Ootah's Lucky Day.* Illustrated by Mamoru Funai. HarperCollins, 1970.
The day he went hunting proved to be Ootah's lucky day!

Steiner, Barbara. *The Whale Brother.* Illustrated by Gretchen Will Mayo. Walker, 1988.
Watching whales with an artist's eye.

NON-FICTION

Brikenden, Jack. *We Live in Canada.* Bookwright Press, 1985.
Interviews with 28 people from a broad spectrum of Canadian society.

Burton, Robert. *Arctic Animals.* Illustrated with color photographs. Oxford Scientific Films, 1991. (Gr. K-3)
Beautiful color photographs with short text describing various Arctic animals.

Ryder, Joanne. *White Bear, Ice Bear.* Illustrated by Michael Rothman. Morrow, 1989.
A child becomes a white bear in the Arctic for one day.

Simon, Seymour. *Icebergs and Glaciers.* Morrow, 1987.
Describes the formation, movement and types of glaciers and icebergs.

Wombat Stew

by Marcia Vaughan. Illustrated by Pamela Lofts.

A Story About Animals of Australia

Some of the most unusual animals in the world are found in Australia. A few of these animals are:

1. platypus	2. emu	3. lizard
4. echidna	5. dingo	6. wombat

Work with a partner or small group. Guess which animal goes with each description below. Put the number of the animal on the line after each description. Then read or listen to the booktalk to support or deny your guesses.

A. I have a bill like a duck and a tail like a beaver. ______

B. I have a long neck, two legs and feathers. ______

C. I have a long tongue used for catching flies and my body has a skin like a snake. ______

D. I have quills like a porcupine and a long snout for eating bugs. ______

E. I look like a dog and my name rhymes with bingo. ______

F. A small furry animal that comes out at night. ______

Answers: (found in booktalk) A. platypus B. emu C. lizard D. echidna E. dingo F. wombat

Wombat Stew

by Marcia Vaughan. Illustrated by Pamela Lofts.

Silver Burdette, 1986

Booktalk

Australia

One day a wild dog or dingo catches a furry wombat and decides to make a wombat stew. Along comes a duck-billed platypus who suggests that the stew would taste better if dingo added globs of mud. The longnecked emu arrives and wants to add feathers. Lizard, who uses his long tongue to catch flies, wants more flies added to the stew. Then echidna arrives and says no stew would be worth eating unless it had lots and lots of bugs. Finally the stew is ready. Dingo is about to toss the wombat into the pot when the other animals tell him to stop...he has forgotten the most important thing. What do you suppose dingo has forgotten? Will wombat really end up in the stew? To find out, read *Wombat Stew* by Marcia Vaughan.

About the Author/Illustrator

Marcia Vaughan was born in Tacoma, Washington. She has always loved books and became a school librarian so that she could help children to love books, too. In 1988 she moved to New South Wales, Australia where she continued to work as a school librarian and as an author. Among her other titles are *Ships, Boats and Things That Float*, *The Lucky Fun Book* and *As Far as That.*

About Australia

Australia is an island continent made up of rain forests, deserts and the bush. The land has a variety of birds, reptiles and different kinds of mammals. Most of the people of Australia live along the coasts. Sheep farming and mining are important occupations for the people on the "outback" or away from the coastal regions. When the first English settlers came to Australia they found the native people or Aborigines who still live there today.

Wombat Stew

by Marcia Vaughan. Illustrated by Pamela Lofts.

A Problem to Solve

Suppose you were one of the other animals in the story. How might you save wombat from being put into the stew? List your ideas on the lines in the box below.

	Criteria for judging each idea				
Ideas for Saving Wombat	**Fast**	**Low Cost**	**Safe**	**Effective**	**Total**
1. Tell dingo that wombat stew does not taste good.	**3**	**3**	**2**	**1**	**9**
2.					
3.					
4.					

Score each idea as follows: 1 = No 2 = maybe 3 = yes.
Total the scores for each idea. The idea with the highest score is the one to try.
The best idea is ____

____

Now finish the story to see what idea the author has for saving wombat from the stew.

Wombat Stew
by Marcia Vaughan. Illustrated by Pamela Lofts.

Australian Animal Chant

Australian animals!
  Platypus
  Emu
  Lizard
  Echidna
  Dingo
  Kangaroo
These are just a few
  Duck-billed
  Feathers
  Scaly skin
  Prickly Spines
  Wild Dog
  Pockets
What a mixed-up zoo!
Stand and Shout
Bring them out
Australian animals!

Wombat Stew
by Marcia Vaughan. Illustrated by Pamela Lofts.

Here is a data bank about the wombat.

Data Bank - Wombat

Lives
Australia
in a burrow

Eats
roots
vegetables
leaves

What It Does
carries its young in a pouch
makes an affectionate pet
digs large earth burrows
comes out only at night

What It Has
a pouch
tough hide
long fur
sharp claws
small ears
whiskers

Looks Like
2 - 3 feet long
yellow/black color
furry possum

Song Pattern. Sing to the tune of "London Bridge"
(Using information from the data bank)

Wombats eat both roots and leaves
Roots and leaves
Roots and leaves
Wombats come out just at night
And dig burrows.

Choose another Australian animal. Create a data bank for the animal similar to the one about wombats.

Use the information from your data bank to write a song.

More Picture Story Books About Australia

PICTURE BOOKS

Cox, David. *Bossyboots*. Crown Publishers, 1985.
Abilgail is a bit overwhelming for the other stagecoach riders but when the coach is held up, Abigail knows just what to do.

Dumbleton, Mike. *Dial-A-Croc*. Illustrated by Ann James. Orchard Books, 1991.
Vanessa captures a crocodile in the outback and rents him out for a variety of hilarious jobs.

Fox, Mem. *Koala Lou*. Illustrated by Pamela Lofts. Ian Drakeford Publishing Pty. Ltd., 1988
Koala Lou tries to win the attention of her mother by entering the bush Olympics.

Fox, Mem. *Possum Magic*. Illustrated by Julie Vivas. Penguin Books Australia. 1983
Grandma Poss and Hush travel around Australia trying to find a food that will make Hush visible again.

Park, Ruth. *The Gigantic Balloon*. Illustrated by Kilmeny Deborah Neland. Williams Collins Publishers, 1975
A shop assistant's dream comes true when a gigantic balloon arrives and he becomes the balloonist.

Thiele, Colin. *Farmer Schultz's Ducks*. Illustrated by Mary Milton. HarperCollins, 1986.
A story set in South Australia on the Onkaparinga which tells the troubles of one farmer and his ducks when city life moves in.

Tulloch, Richard. *Rain For Christmas*. Illustrated by Wayne Harris. Cambridge, 1990.
Set in the rain-parched Australian outback, a young girl asks for rain rather than presents for Christmas.

Wilson, Barbara Ker. *Acacia Terrace*. Illustrated by David Fielding. Scholastic Hardcover, 1990.
A true account of a Sydney, Australia neighborhood and the ever changing lives of the different families who lived there from the 1860s to the present.

NON-FICTION

Wheatley, Nadia. *My Place*. Illustrated by Donna Rawlins. Kane/Miller, 1988.
Beginning in 1988 and going back 200 years, here is a history of Australia told by generations of children who lived in one particular place. Rich in detail with maps showing 200 years of change.

Our Country Australia by Andrew Kelly with photographs by David Power, Bookwright Press, 1991.
This is a book which explains the activities, occupations, recreations, industries, religions, cultures, foods, and wildlife of Australia on an elementary level.

The Land and People of Australia by Godfrey Blunden, Lippincott, 1972.
This book examines the geographical layout and discusses the people of Australia and their way of life.

Tattercoats

Collected and edited by Joseph Jacobs.

Illustrated by Margot Tomes. G. P. Putnam's, 1989

Booktalk

Great Britain

In a Palace by the sea an old lord sat day after day. His white beard grew so long that it tangled around his chair. He was all alone except for servants and a granddaughter he hated bitterly, for her mother, his only daughter had died at her birth. So the child grew up with no one to care for her and was given only scraps from the kitchen and clothes from the rag bag. But when she grew sad she had only to find the gooseherd boy who would play on his pipes and cheer her up.

Now it happened that the King was to give a great ball and from the ladies attending would find a bride for the Prince. The gooseherd proposed that they go together to see the fine palace. As they were piping along the way, a well dressed stranger joined them. The more the pipes were played, the more he fell in love with Tattercoats. The stranger begged her to come to the ball but in her tattered clothes she dared not do so. But the pipes of the gooseherd that could cheer her and wipe away her tears had other magic as well. And at the ball there will be some unexpected surprises as Tattercoats and the stranger meet once again.

About the Author

Joseph Jacobs was an Englishman who collected folktales and rewrote them in language that would appeal to children. His first collection of tales, *English Fairy Tales*, was published in 1890. These tales were among the first that were brought to the United States and are very familiar to most children today. The collection includes: "The Little Red Hen", "The Three Bears" and the "Three Little Pigs" among many other favorite tales. Other collections by Jacobs include *Celtic Fairy Tales* published in 1899.

Tattercoats

Collected and edited by Joseph Jacobs.

Illustrated by Margot Tomes. G. P. Putnam's, 1989

Performing the Booktalk

Speaking Parts:	Narrator One, Narrator Two, Gooseheard, The Old Lord, Tattercoats, The Stranger, King
Narrator One:	In a palace by the sea an old Lord
Lord:	sat day after day.
Narrator One:	His white beard
Lord:	grew so long
Narrator One:	that it tangled around his chair. He was all alone
Lord:	except for servants and a granddaughter
Narrator One:	he hated bitterly, for her mother, his only daughter had died at her birth.
Narrator Two:	So the child grew up with no one to care for her
Tattercoats:	and was given only scraps from the kitchen and clothes from the ragbag.
Narrator Two:	But when she grew sad she had only
Tattercoats:	to find the gooseherd boy who would play on his pipes
Gooseherd:	and cheer her up.
Narrator One:	Now it happened that the King
King:	was to give a great ball and from the ladies attending would find a bride for the Prince.
Narrator Two:	The gooseherd proposed that
Gooseherd:	they go together to see the fine palace.
Narrator Two:	As they were piping along the way, a well-dressed stranger

Performing the Booktalk (continued)

Stranger: joined them.

Narrator One: The more the pipes were played, the more he

Stranger: fell in love with Tattercoats.

Narrator One: The stranger begged her

Stranger: to come to the ball

Narrator Two: but in her tattered clothes she

Tattercoats: dared not do so.

Narrator One: But the pipes of the gooseherd

Gooseherd: that could cheer her and wipe away her tears

Narrator One: had other magic as well.

Narrator Two: And at the ball there will be some unexpected surprises as Tattercoats and the stranger

Tattercoats & Stranger: meet once again.

Responding to the Booktalk

Work in groups of three or four. List as many ways as you can that the story of *Tattercoats* is like the story of *Cinderella*.

1. ______________________________
2. ______________________________
3. ______________________________
4. ______________________________
5. ______________________________
6. ______________________________
7. ______________________________

Creating Sentences

Work in groups of three. On small, separate pieces of paper write words you think of when looking at this picture. Use nouns, verbs adjectives and adverbs. After ten minutes, arrange your words in a sentence to describe the picture. (You do not have to use all the words.) You can add prepositions and the words "a", "an" and "the" if you need them in your sentence.

Read your sentence aloud to the class.

About the British Isles

The island of Great Britain, just off the coast of continental Europe, includes England, Scotland, Wales and Northern Ireland. The British have a deep love for their land and the sea. The land ranges from the hills and mountains of Wales to the Highlands of Scotland to the green and rolling plains of England. The Queen of England is Elizabeth II who reigns but does not rule. Ministers of Parliament actually rule the country. If you visited London, the capital city, you would see ships from every land sail to and from the Port of London. You could take a tour of the Tower of London and see the royal jewels. You might also watch the changing of the guard at Buckingham Palace. You could go horseback riding on Rotten Row and see the statue of Peter Pan at Kensington Gardens.

TAKE A POLL! What would members of your class most like to do in London?

Students surveyed	See the changing of the guard	Go horse-back riding	See the Royal jewels	See the statue of Peter Pan
A				
B				
C				
D				
E				
F				
G				
H				

The favorite thing most class members polled was

____

More Folktales from the British Isles

PICTURE BOOKS

Bishop, Gavin. *Chicken Licken*. Illustrated by the author. Oxford, 1984.
Chicken Licken discovers the danger in listening to Foxy Loxy.

Brown, Marcia. *Dick Whittington and His Cat*. Illustrated by the author. Scribner, 1950.
A realistic tale of a popular British hero.

Cauley, Lorinda Bryan. *Jack and the Beanstalk*. Illustrated by the author. Putnam's, 1983.
An adventurous boy climbs a beanstalk to confront a giant.

Cooper, Susan. *The Silver Cow*. Illustrated by Warwick Hutton. Atheneum, 1983.
Fairies take revenge against a greedy father.

de la Mare, Walter. *Mollie Whuppie*. Illustrated by Errol Le Cain. Farrar, Straus & Giroux, 1983.
The tale of a clever girl who tricks a giant.

Godden, Rumer. *The Old Woman Who Lived in a Vinegar Bottle*. Illustrated by Mairi Hedderwick. Viking, 1972.
An old woman is happy in her vinegar bottle house until she saves the life of a fish and is granted her every wish.

Jeffers, Susan. *Wild Robin*. Illustrated by the author. Dutton, 1976.
A young girl must have courage to rescue her wayward brother.

Kellogg, Steven. *Chicken Little*. Illustrated by the author. Morrow, 1985.
Chicken Little is hit on the head by an acorn and is convinced the sky is falling.

Ness, Evaline. *Tom Tit Tot*. Illustrated by the author. Scribner's, 1965.
The English version of *Rumplestiltskin*.

Shub, Elizabeth (translator) *The Fisherman and His Wife*. Illustrated by Monica Laimgruber. Greenwillow 1978.
A fisherman is granted wishes by a magic fish until his greedy wife asks for too much.

Zemach. Margot. *The Fisherman and His Wife*. Translated by Randall Jarrell. Illustrated by the author. Farrar, Straus & Giroux, 1980.
Another illustrated version of this famous tale.

NON-FICTION

James, Ian. *Inside Great Britain*. Photographs by Chris Fairclough. Watts, 1988. (Gr. 3-4)
Looks at Britain's history, culture, cities, family life, food, sports, art and future challenges.

Langley Andrew. *Passport to Great Britain*. Watts, 1986. (Gr. 4-6)
Looks at many current and past aspects of British life and describes modern daily life there.

Munro, Roxie. *The Inside-outside Book of London*. Dutton, 1989. (Gr. K-3)
Illustrations with brief captions of noted London sights including the British Museum, Houses of Parliament, Tower of London, Waterloo Station, St. Paul's Cathedral and others.

St. John, Letty. *A Family in England*. Photographs by Nigel Harvey. Lerner, 1988. (Gr. 3-4)
Describes the homes, schools, amusements, customs and work of a thirteen-year-old boy living in a small village in England.

The Ghost Horse of the Mounties

by Sean O'Huigin. Illustrated by Barry Moser.

David R. Godine, Publishers, 1991

Booktalk

Canada

This legend told in verse begins on a black summer's night on a lonely Canadian plain. Six Mounties are watching over 250 wild horses when a terrible storm beats down upon the camp. The horses stampede and in the rush to capture them, one young man is tossed aside and trampled. His own horse sees his master fall, then takes off in fright with the others. The young Mountie dies of his injuries and the only horse which is not recaptured is his. The horse roams the plains and after many years feels a strange force pulling him toward a weathered mound of earth with a broken wooden cross. The horse has at last found its master.

About the Author/Illustrator

Sean O' Huigin is a Canadian poet who tells this tale in verse. His poetry books are popular with children since many are filled with humor. A favorite is *Scary Poems for Rotten Kids*. "The Ghost Horse of the Mounties" is a serious and dramatic retelling of an incident from the history of the Royal Canadian Mounted Police.

About the Royal Canadian Mounted Police

In 1869 it was very difficult for a family to travel north in Canada to settle in the vast Northwest Territory. It was a wild region, 900 miles long and 900 miles wide. Those wishing to claim land there by settling and building homes were often attacked by wild bands of criminals. The Royal Canadian Mounted Police was established to bring law and order to the land. By 1873 the force was operating throughout the land. They kept law and order, carried mail, reported on crop and road damage and even fought forest fires. The fame of the Mounties has spread throughout the world. Few groups are better than the Mounties in bringing law and order to the people and making the land safe.

The Ghost Horse of the Mounties
by Sean O'Huigin. Illustrated by Barry Moser.
David R. Godine, Publishers, 1991

Performing the Booktalk

Speaking Parts: Narrator One, Narrator Two, Mounties, Young Man, Horse

Narrator One: This legend told in verse begins on a black summer's night on a lonely Canadian plain.

Narrator Two: Six Mounties

Mounties: are watching over 250 wild horses when a terrible storm beats down upon the camp.

Narrator Two: The horses stampede, and in a rush to capture them one young man

Young Man: is tossed aside and trampled.

Narrator Two: His own horse sees his master fall then

Horse: takes off in fright with the others.

Narrator One: The young Mountie dies of his injuries

Narrator Two: and the only horse which is not recaptured is his. The horse

Horse: roams the plains and after many years feels a strange force

Narrator One: pulling him toward a weathered mound of earth with a broken wooden cross.

Mounties: The horse has at last found its master.

Responding To The Booktalk

"Puss in Boots" is another tale about an animal and its master. Can you find ways that this legend, *The Ghost Horse of the Mounties*, and "Puss in Boots" are alike?

The Ghost Horse of the Mounties

The "I Have, Who Has" Game

Cut apart the cards and distribute randomly. The person with the card with two stars (**) reads the "WHO HAS" portion of the card. The person who has a card with the correct response reads the "I HAVE" portion of his or her card; then reads the "WHO HAS" portion of the card. The game continues until all cards are read.

THE GHOST HORSE OF THE MOUNTIES

I Have:	The horse found the grave of the Mountie.
** Start here:	
Who Has:	When did the legend of the Ghost Horse begin?

I Have:	The Ghost Horse legend began on a black summer's night.
Who Has:	What were the Mounties doing on this black summer's night?

I Have:	The Mounties were watching over 250 horses when a storm came up.
Who Has:	What did the horses and the Mounties do when the storm came?

I Have:	The horses bolted in fear and the Mounties tried to catch them.
Who Has:	What happened to one young Mountie and his horse?

I Have:	One young Mountie was killed and his horse roamed the plains for years.
Who Has:	How were the Mountie and his horse reunited?

Which Would You Rather Be?

Choose One:

A Mountie　　　　　　A Wild Horse

Look carefully at the pattern in the box.

"If I Were" Pattern

1. Name the thing you want to be

2. Where is it found?

3. One thing it would do for someone else
4. A second thing it would do
5. Repeat the first line

If I were a ______________________________
On (or in) ______________________________
I would ________________________________
And ___________________________________
If I were a ______________________________

Choose another person or animal you would like to be.
Write an "If I Were" poem about that person or animal.

If I were a ______________________________

On (or in) ______________________________

I would ________________________________

And ___________________________________

If I were a ______________________________

Create A Canada Alphabet Book

Read about Canada in the encyclopedia or in other books in your school or public library. Find one word for each letter of the alphabet that will tell something about the country. Put together a class ABC Book of Canada with each student writing about and illustrating one word.

A	Arctic Circle	N	
B	Beauty	O	
C		P	
D		Q	
E		R	
F		S	
G		T	
H		U	
I		V	
J		W	
K		X	
L		Y	
M		Z	

A is for Canada. (Why?)	Part of the land of Canada is in the **Arctic** Circle
B is for Canada. (Why?)	Over one million tourists annually enjoy the **Beauty** of Canada's mountains and waterways.

More Picture Books Set in Canada

PICTURE BOOKS

Andrews, Jan. *Very Last First Time*. Illustrated by Ian Wallace. Macmillan Publishing, 1985.
Eva Padlyat was exploring the seabed for mussels. When her candle went out she decided it was her very last first time.

Blades, Ann. *Mary of Mile 18*. Illustrated by the author. Tundra Books of Montreal, 1971.
Any child can relate to the story of young Mary Fehr who longs to keep a wolf pup that her father won't allow.

Climo, Lindee. *Chester's Barn*. Tundra Books, 1982.
Chester takes care of all the animals in the barn making sure they get fed and get to run everyday. He pays especially close attention to Cow Ma who has a healthy calf at the end of the story.

Holling, Holling C. *Paddle to the Sea*. Illustrated by the author. Houghton Mifflin, 1984.
A young boy sets off in a canoe to reach the Atlantic which was far from his home. After finally making it through many obstacles he earns the name Paddle-to-the-Sea.

Ward, Lynn. *The Biggest Bear*. Illustrated by the author. Houghton Mifflin, 1952.
This story tells of a young boy who befriends a bear cub.

Ward, Lynn. *Nic of the Woods*. Illustrated by the author. Houghton Mifflin, 1965.
Young Davy thinks Nic is the smartest dog ever, until Davy and his family take Nic on a vacation into the Canadian woods where Nic finds all sorts of thing he needs to learn.

Waterton, Betty. *A Salmon for Simon*. Illustrated by Ann Blades. Atheneum, 1978.
Simon wanted to catch a salmon. He tried everyday, but when he finally did, he didn't feel happy. Simon decided to let the fish go free and not to fish for salmon anymore.

Winter, Jeanette. *Follow the Drinking Gourd*. Illustrated by the author. Alfred A. Knopf, 1988.
An old man was helping slaves escape. After many weeks they stepped on Canadian soil and tasted freedom for the first time.

NON-FICTION

Bender, Lionel. *People and Places of Canada*. Illustrated by Ann Savage. Silver Burdett, 1988.
This book is about the people of Canada who mostly are of French and British origin. It also tells about the beautiful tourist sights in Canada.

Breckenden, Jack. *Canada*. Illustrated by Malcolm Walker. Bookwright, 1989.
The history, geography, cultures, climate and people of Canada.

Jacket cover illustration by Ed Young, © 1989. Used with permission of Philomel Books.

Lon Po Po: A Red Riding Hood Story From China

Translated & illustrated by Ed Young

Philomel, 1989

Booktalk

China

Long, long ago, a good woman lived contentedly with her three daughters, Shang, Tao and Paotze, in the countryside of northern China. But one day she had to leave to visit their granny, so she warned the children to close the door tightly and to latch it.

Soon after, to their surprise, there was a knock at the door and a voice saying it was their granny, their Po Po. What could the children do but let her in? But what a low voice she had, what thorny hands and what a hairy face! To discover how three little girls outwit a wicked, wicked wolf, read *Lon Po Po*.

About the Author/Illustrator

Ed Young was born and grew up in China. He came to the United States and studied at the University of Illinois, the Art Center of Los Angeles, and the Pratt Institute of New York. He has illustrated many books for children.

About China

Mainland China is larger than the United States and covers three and a half million square miles. About one billion people live there so the cities are very crowded. In fact most people travel on bicycles since there is not room for many cars. Children in China start school at age seven. Favorite sports are basketball, volley ball, gymnastics and swimming. One of the biggest holidays is the Spring Festival known as the Chinese New Year. The most commonly eaten foods in China are fish and rice.

Lon Po Po: A Red Riding Hood Story From China

Translated & illustrated by Ed Young

Philomel, 1989

Performing the Booktalk

Speaking Parts: Narrator, The Good Woman, The Three Daughters, The Wolf (Po Po)

Narrator:	Long, long ago, a good woman
Good Woman:	lived contentedly
Narrator:	with her three daughters:
Daughters:	Shang, Tao and Paotze,
Narrator:	in the countryside of northern China. But one day she
Good Woman:	had to leave to visit their granny
Narrator:	so she
Good Woman:	warned the children to close the door tightly and latch it.
Narrator:	Soon after, to their surprise,
Daughters:	there was a knock at the door and a voice saying
Wolf:	it was their granny, their Po Po.
Narrator:	What could the children do but
Daughters:	let her in? But what a
Wolf:	low voice
Daughters:	she had, what
Wolf:	thorny hands
Daughters:	and what a
Wolf:	hairy face!

Performing the Booktalk (continued)

Narrator:	To discover how
Daughters:	three little girls
Narrator:	outwit a
Wolf:	wicked, wicked wolf,
Narrator:	Read *Lon Po Po.*

Responding to the Booktalk

List as many way as you can that this story and the story of *Little Red Riding Hood* are alike.

Play the Mystery Word Game

Here are some clues that are important to the story, *Lon Po Po.* To play the game:

1. One person is the clue caller. That person asks for a volunteer to give a number between one and five. The clue caller then reads the word for the number given.
2. If the volunteer cannot guess the thing that the word describes, the clue caller asks for another volunteer to give a different number and reads the clue for that number. The game continues until a correct guess is made or all numbers are used.

ROUND ONE	ROUND TWO	ROUND THREE	ROUND FOUR
1. tall	1. round	1. soft	1. fur
2. leaves	2. woven	2. tender	2. claws
3. branches	3. empty	3. grow	3. teeth
4. bark	4. handle	4. tree	4. thorny
5. nuts	5. large	5. magic	5. hairy
(Gingko Tree)	(basket)	(Gingko Nuts)	(wolf)

Lon Po Po

Time For Skills

To the Teacher

Make an overhead transparency of the visual on page 37 or show the cover of the book. Place students in small groups of three or four. Pass out to each group a small 'post it' pad or have each group tear small pieces of paper (about 2" X 2"). Place the overhead visual on the projector and instruct the groups as follows.

1. Taking turns in your group, give words related to the picture. Name words, action words, describing words are important.

2. When a word is given the secretary for each group writes the word on one small piece of paper and puts it in a pile.

3. Your first objective is to get a large pile of words.

4. After about 20 minutes (when the teacher or leader calls STOP), arrange any words you choose from your word pile into a sentence that describes the picture. You may add prepositions as needed and the noun determiners, a, an and the.

5. Be prepared to read aloud your sentence to the class.

More Skills

1. Look carefully at the illustration.

   A. Write a declarative sentence about the picture.
   B. Write an interrogative sentence about the picture.
   C. Write an imperative sentence about the picture.
   D. Write an exclamatory sentence about the picture.
   E. Write a sentence about the picture that contains two common nouns.

More Tales About China

PICTURE BOOKS

Bishop, Claire Huchet. *The Five Chinese Brothers*. Illustrated by Kurt Wiese Putnam, 1938.
Five identical brothers each possess a superhuman trait to outwit the executioner.

Lattimore, Deborah. *The Dragon's Robe*. HarperCollins, 1990.
Kwan Yin weaves a robe for the emperor and saves the city.

Leaf, Margaret. *Eyes of the Dragon*. Illustrated by Ed Young. HarperCollins/Lothrop, 1987.
When the magistrate insists that a dragon painting include eyes, the dragon comes to life.

Morris, Winifred *The Future of Yen-Tzu*. Illustrated by Friso Henstra. Atheneum 1992.
A farmer's son discovers the future can change from one moment to the next.

Mosel, Arlele. *Tikki Tikki Tembo*. Illustrated by Blair Lent. Holt, 1968.
When the eldest son fell in the well and most of the time was spent in saying his name, the Chinese decided to give their children shorter names.

Pattison, Darcy. *The River Dragon*. Illustrated by Jean and Mou Sien Tseng. HarperCollins/ Lothrop, 1991.
A weak man outwits a powerful dragon to cross the bridge to his bride's home.

Rappaport, Doreen. *The Journey of Meng*. Illustrated by Yang Ming-Yi. Dial Books, 1991.
A brave Chinese woman sets out to aid her husband who is building the Great Wall.

Tompert Ann. *Grandfather Tang's Story*. Illustrated by Robert Andrew Parker. Crown Books, 1990.
Grandfather Tang and Little Soo are playing a game with tangrams to tell a story.

Wang, Rosalind C. *The Fourth Question: A Chinese Folktale*. Illustrated by Ju-Hong Chen. Holiday House, 1991.
Yee-Lee learns an old lesson: doing good deeds brings happiness and rewards.

Yolen, Jane. *The Emperor and the Kite*. Illustrated by Ed Young. Philomel, 1988.
The emperor's daughter frees her father from imprisonment by means of a kite.

Zimelman, Nathan. *The Great Adventure of Wo Ti*. Illustrated by Julie Dowling. Macmillan, 1992.
Wo Ti longs to see the outside world until danger enters the palace grounds.

NON-FICTION

Feinstein Steve. *China in Pictures* (Visual Geography Series) Lerner, 1989.
An overview of China in photographs.

Kalman, Bobbie. *China, The Culture* (Lands Peoples and Cultures Series) Crabtree Publishing Co., 1989.
This book focuses on the arts, food beliefs, festivals and games of China.

Pitkann, Matti A. *The Children of China*. Carolrhoda Books, 1990.
One child from each major area of China is depicted in daily life.

Puss in Boots
by Charles Perrault
Fairy Tales, 1697

Modern picture book versions include:

Puss in Boots Illustrated by Marcia Brown. Scribner's, 1952
Puss in Boots Illustrated by Paul Galdone. Seabury, 1976
Puss in Boots Illustrated by Lorinda Bryan Cauley. Harcourt, 1986
Puss in Boots Illustrated by Fred Marcellino. Farrar, 1990
Puss in Boots Illustrated by Tony Ross. Delacorte, 1981
Puss in Boots and Other Stories, Illustrated by Anne Rockwell, Macmillan, 1988

Booktalk

France

When the miller died, his oldest son received the mill, his middle son received a donkey, and his youngest son received a cat. The youngest son had no idea how to make a living with the cat except to kill it and eat it and make a hat of its fur. The cat, hearing this, promised that if the boy would give him boots and a sack that he would make the young man wealthy. Using the sack the cat manages to catch rabbits and partridges and take them to the king from his master the "Marquis of Carabas." When the king and his party are out riding one morning the cat tells the boy to take off his clothes and jump into the river. As the coach passes by the cat calls to the king to save his master who has been robbed and is in danger of drowning. The boy is rescued and falls in love with the king's daughter. But how can he convince the king that he is worthy of her? Leave it to *Puss in Boots* to solve the problem!

About the Author

In 1697 Charles Perrault was a distinguished member of the French Academy. At that time fairy tales were extremely popular and being told and retold in the Court of Louis XIV. Perrault collected and wrote down many of these tales and published them in a small volume of fairy tales. Other tales in this first collection included *Cinderella, Red Riding Hood* and *The Sleeping Beauty.*

Puss in Boots
by Charles Perrault

Performing the Booktalk

Speaking Parts: Narrator One, Narrator Two, Oldest Son, Middle Son, Youngest Son, Cat, King

Narrator One:	When the miller died, his oldest son
Oldest Son:	received the mill,
Narrator Two:	his middle son
Middle Son:	received a donkey,
Narrator One:	and his youngest son
Youngest Son:	received a cat.
Narrator One:	The youngest son had no idea
Youngest Son:	how to make a living with the cat except to kill it and eat it and make a hat of its fur.
Narrator Two:	The cat, hearing this, promised that if the boy would give him boots and a sack that he would
Cat:	make the young man wealthy. Using the sack
Narrator Two:	the cat manages to catch
Cat:	rabbits and partridges and take them to the king
Narrator One:	from his master, the "Marquis of Carabas." When the king and his party
King:	are out riding one morning,
Narrator Two:	the cat tells the boy
Cat:	to take off his clothes and jump into the river.

Puss in Boots
Performing the Booktalk (continued)

Narrator Two:	As the coach passes by, the cat
Cat:	calls to the king
Narrator One:	to save his master
Cat:	who has been robbed and is in danger of drowning.
Narrator One:	The boy
Youngest Son:	is rescued and falls in love with the king's daughter.
Narrator One:	But how can he convince the king that he is
Youngest Son:	worthy of her?
All:	Leave it to *Puss in Boots* to solve the problem.

Responding to the Booktalk

Many fairy tales have similar characters, settings and plots. Another tale where playing a trick on someone was important is *The Three Little Pigs.*

Work together in groups of three or four. Each group should have a secretary or recorder to write the main ideas of the group. In five minutes list all the ways you can that *Puss in Boots* and *The Three Little Pigs* are alike. Share your list with other groups.

Puss in Boots
Learning Skills With Story Strips

<u>Directions:</u> Cut the strips apart. Give a set of strips to a small group of three or four students. Students work together to put the strips in correct order to tell the story. Then students work together to add correct capitalization and punctuation. When a group has completed its task, a monitor or teacher can check for correctness.

---

long long ago a miller died and left his

---

youngest son a cat who promised to make the

---

young man wealthy the cat caught rabbits and gave them

---

to the king from his master then the boy pretended

---

to drown and the kings men saved him and took him to

---

the palace where the boy fell in love

---

with the kings daughter

---

but how can he convince the king he is worthy of her

Puss in Boots
What Would You Do?

Cut out the incident cards below and select one for each blank space on the storyboard. (You will not use all of the incident cards.) When the storyboard is completed, tell how you would solve the youngest son's problem.

Story Board

1. Characters: Youngest son Puss in Boots King's Daughter	4. Place an incident card here
2. Place an incident card here	5. Place an incident card here
3. The youngest son wants the daughter to marry him but thinks she won't if she finds out he is poor.	6. And they were married and lived happily ever after.

Incident Cards

he finds a magic ring	an earthquake destroys the king's palace
money is not important to happiness	an army from another kingdom approaches
it starts to rain	an invitation to a fishing contest arrives
the king's daughter becomes ill	Puss in Boots finds a bag of gold

Puss in Boots
About France

Here are words you would hear in France.

Paris	Tour de France	Mont Blanc
Louis XIV	escargot	bon jour

Work with a friend to see if you can unscramble the words to answer each question below.

1. What is the capital of France? (SIRAP) ____________________
2. How do you say 'hello' in French? (NOB ROUJ) ________________
3. Name a famous French King. (SIUOL XIV) ____________________
4. Name the highest point in France.(TNOM BLCAN) _____________
5. French people like to eat this. (GTORACSE) ________________
6. A famous French bicycle race is (OTUR DE ANCEFR)

   ____

Support or deny your guesses by reading the poem below.

HAIL TO FRANCE!

I see Paris
Capital of France
I would go there if I had the chance.
I've heard of Mont Blanc
The highest place,
The Tour de France is a famous bike race.
"Bon Jour," says the waiter.
"Will you have some escargot?"
He said "Hello" and offered you some slimy snails to go.
Louis XIV was a famous French King
The flag is red and white and blue
As Hail to France we sing.

Answers: 1. Paris 2. Bon Jour 3. Louis XIV 4. Mont Blanc 5. escargot 6. Tour de France

More Picture Story Books About France

PICTURE BOOKS

Agee, John. *The Incredible Painting of Felix Clousseau*. Farrar, Straus & Giroux, 1990.
An unknown painter becomes an overnight sensation when his paintings imitate life too well by quacking, crawling and erupting all over Paris.

Bemelmans, Ludwig. *Madeline*. Viking Press, 1939.
A rhyming story about Madeline, one of twelve little girls, who has her appendix taken out and her friends want theirs taken out too!

DeBrunhoff, Jean. *The Story of Babar: The Little Elephant*. Random House, 1933.
Babar runs away to Paris, but then returns to become King of the Elephants.

Dillon, Diane. *Where's Our Mama*? Illustrated by Diane Goode. Dutton, 1991.
Children become separated from their mother at a busy Paris train station and a friendly policeman tries to help them find her.

Fatio, Louise. *The Happy Lion*. Illustrated by Roger Duvoisin. McGraw Hill, 1954.
A French lion finds his cage door open, so he takes a walk, much to the surprise of the people in the town.

Hague, Michael. *Cinderella and Other Tales From Perrault*. Henry Holt & Co., 1989.
An illustrated collection of Perrault tales including some lesser known tales.

Hastings, Selina. *Reynard the Fox*. Illustrated by Graham Percy. Tambourine Books, 1991.
No animal is safe from the sharp teeth and sharp wits of the fox.

Haviland, Virginia. *Favorite Fairy Tales Told in France*. Little Brown, 1959.
An easy-to-read collection that includes "The Twelve Dancing Princesses", "Puss in Boots", "Beauty and the Beast," "Sleeping Beauty in the Wood" and "Drakestail."

Ungerer, Tomi. *Allumette*. Four Winds Press, 1974.
An orphan who is granted her every wish finds she has too much and gives it away to the needy.

NON-FICTION - FRANCE

Harris, Jonathan. *The Land and People of France*. Lippincott, 1989.
This book describes the history, geography, government, economy, culture and people of France.

James, Ian. *Inside France*. Franklin Watts, 1988.
A brief introduction to the land and the people of France including their history and their future.

Snow White and Rose Red
by Jakob and Wilhelm Grimm
Illustrated by Gennady Spirin. Philomel Books, 1992

Booktalk

Germany

A BEAR! when they opened the door of their cottage one stormy winter evening, Snow White and Rose Red were astonished, and a bit frightened, to see a huge shaggy bear standing outside. His fur was covered with snow, and he seemed half frozen so they took pity on him and invited him to warm himself by the fire. He proved to be a gentle creature and came often to visit during the winter...only to disappear mysteriously in the spring. But he was no ordinary bear, as they were soon to discover and he found a surprising way to repay *Snow White and Rose Red* for their kindness to him.

About the Authors

Snow White and Rose Red appeared in the earliest collection of tales gathered and written down by the brothers Grimm. After these two brothers finished law school they spent many weeks searching and writing down old tales from the German countryside. Until that time (about 1812) the tales had only been told and never written. Jakob was a language scholar and was interested in the history of the tales and found many similarities of the German tales with early Greek myths. Without the work of these two brothers in collecting the tales, many might not be so well known today.

Snow White and Rose Red

by Jakob and Wilhelm Grimm

Illustrated by Gennady Spirin. Philomel Books, 1992

Performing the Booktalk

Speaking Parts: Narrator, Snow White, Rose Red, Bear

Narrator:	A BEAR! When they opened the door of their cottage one stormy winter evening, Snow White and Rose Red were astonished
Both Girls:	and a bit frightened, to see a huge bear
Bear:	standing outside.
Narrator:	His fur
Bear:	was covered with snow
Narrator:	and he seemed half frozen so they
Both Girls:	took pity on him
Snow White:	and invited him to warm himself by the fire.
Narrator:	He proved to be a gentle creature
Bear:	and came often to visit during the winter, only to disappear mysteriously in the spring.
Narrator:	But he was no ordinary bear as they were
Both Girls:	soon to discover,
Narrator:	and he found
Bear:	a surprising way
Narrator:	to repay Snow White and Rose Red for their kindness to him.

Responding to the Booktalk

In small groups of three or four discuss the following question: How is the story of *Beauty and the Beast* like the story of *Snow White and Rose Red*. One person in the group should be the secretary to note the group's main ideas. Think of as many ways as you can that these two stories are alike.

Snow White and Rose Red

The "I Have, Who Has" Game

Cut apart the cards and distribute randomly. The person with the card with two stars (**) reads the "WHO HAS" portion of the card. The person who has a card with the correct response reads the "I HAVE" portion of his or her card; then reads the "WHO HAS" portion of the card. The game continues until all cards are read.

I Have:	The bear found a surprising way to repay the girls' kindness.
** Start here:	
Who Has:	What were the girls' names in this story?

I Have:	The girls' names were Snow White and Rose Red.
Who Has:	What strange visitor came to their cottage door?

I Have:	A bear came to the cottage door.
Who Has:	How did the girls feel when they saw a bear at the door?

I Have:	At first the girls were frightened to see a bear at the door.
Who Has:	Why did the girls let the bear into the cottage?

I Have:	The bear proved to be a gentle creature and visited often.
Who Has:	How did the bear repay their kindness?

Snow White and Rose Red

Playing With Words

Directions: Tear a large piece of paper into eight smaller pieces (about the same size). On each small piece of paper write these letters (only one letter on each).

E E N P R S T O

Listen carefully and arrange your letters to make words as the leader reads aloud the following directions:

1. Take four of your letters to make the missing word in this sentence. This is a story about two girls named Snow White and ___ ___ ___ ___ Red.

2. From the word you made, take away one letter and add one letter to add the missing word to this sentence.

   The bear followed his ___ ___ ___ ___ to the cottage.

3. Take away two letters and add two letters to finish this sentence.

   The bear at their door was the strangest sight the girls had ever ___ ___ ___ ___ .

4. Take away two letters and add two letters to tell what the bear needed to do. ___ ___ ___ ___

5. Take away one letter and add two letters to finish this sentence. The girls allowed the bear to ___ ___ ___ ___ ___ the cottage.

6. Add two letters to tell what the bear gave the girls.

   ___ ___ ___ ___ ___ ___ ___

Answers: 1. Rose 2. nose 3. seen 4. rest 5. enter 6. present

About Germany

In 1945 Germany was defeated in World War II and was divided into two nations, East Germany and West Germany. On October 3, 1990 the country again became one nation. The Berlin Wall divided the City of Berlin into East and West Berlin but the government started tearing the wall down in November of 1989. The unified country has a population of about 77 million people. Because the country is small it must import many of the goods and materials the people need. The German people enjoy hiking, reading, gardening and swimming. The Black Forest is the setting for many of the Grimm's fairy tales and the Bavarian Alps also are featured in many stories and films about Germany.

Find the following information about Germany:

Capital City ______________________________

Another large city ______________________________

Three crops ______________________________

Three products ______________________________

Use the information to complete the "Coming Around the Mountain" song below.

She'll be coming from ____________________(Capital) when she comes.
She'll be coming from ____________________ (Large city) when she comes.
She'll bring __________, and __________and __________(Three Crops)
She'll Bring__________, and __________and __________ (Three products)
She'll be coming from GERMANY when she comes.

More Tales From Germany

PICTURE BOOKS

Edens, Cooper. *Beauty and the Beast*. Green Tiger Press, 1989.
The classic tale of the lovely girl and the ugly beast with illustrations from a number of well known artists.

Grimm Brothers. *The Brave Little Tailor*. Translated by Anthea Bell. Illustrated by Eve Tharlet. North-South Books, 1989.

Grimm Brothers. *The Bremen Town Musicians*. Illustrated by Joseph Palecek. Picture Book Studio, 1988.
Four mistreated animal friends set out together and encounter robbers.

Grimm Brothers. *The Fisherman and His Wife*. Illustrated by Alan Marks. Picture Books Studio, 1989.
The fisherman's greedy wife is never satisfied no matter how great the gifts from a magic fish.

Grimm Brothers. *The Frog Prince*. Illustrated by Binette Schroeder. North-South Books, 1989.
A princess makes a promise to an ugly frog who rescues her golden ball from a well.

Grimm Brothers. *The Goose Girl*. Adapted by Anthea Bell. Illustrated by Sabrina Bruntjen. North-South Books, 1988.
A princess and a maid change identities.

Grimm Brothers. *Twelve Dancing Princesses*. Retold by Anne Carter. Illustrated by Anne Dalton. Lippincott, 1989.
Twelve princesses wear out their shoes each night and no one knows why.

Huck, Charlotte. *Princess Furball*. Illustrated by Anita Lobel. Greenwillow Books, 1989.
A princess with a coat of a thousand furs hides her identity from a king.

Zelinsky, Paul O. *Rumplestiltskin*. From the German of the Brothers Grimm. Illustrated by the author. Dutton, 1986.
A miller's daughter makes a foolish promise to a little man who promises to spin straw into gold.

NON-FICTION

Hargrove, Jim. *The Story of the Unification of Germany*. Chicago: Children's Press, 1991. (Gr. 3-4)
This book depicts the events leading to the reunification of East and West Germany through photographs and written text.

Haskins, Jim. *Count Your Way Through Germany*. Illustrated by Helen Byers. Carolrhoda Books, 1990. (Gr. 2-4)
This book uses the numbers one through ten to tell about Germany's language, history, people, traditions and attractions.

The Surprising Things Maui Did

by Jay Williams. Illustrated by Charles Mikolaycak.

Four Winds Press, 1979

Booktalk

United States: Hawaii

Long ago on the Hawaiian Islands, life was very different than it is now. People were cold and hungry and very poor. Then a child named Maui was born.

Because there was not enough food, Maui's mother sent him to live with the Sea God. After six years Maui returned home to his brothers and sisters on the islands, and immediately life began to change.

Maui played his drum, and birds appeared in the trees.

He lifted the sky, so that it lay high in the heavens.

He captured the sun in a net and made it go more slowly so that the land would be warm and the days longer.

But Maui spent a good deal of his time asleep, and despite his wondrous deeds, he was called "Lazy Maui."

When the people of the islands decided they were tired of eating their food raw (or of climbing to the top of the volcano to cook it) they again called on Maui to help them. And despite his laziness, Maui, with the aid of a group of mud hens, caused some *very* surprising things to happen on the islands.

About the Author/Illustrator

The late Jay Williams is the author of many children's books including *Everyone Knows What a Dragon Looks Like*, *The Reward Worth Having* and *The Magic Grandfather* as well as the popular Danny Dunn books.

Charles Mikolaycak was born in Scranton, Pennsylvania and attended Pratt Institute in New York. He is the illustrator of a number of books for young people including *The Man Who Could Call Down Owls*, *Great Wolf* and *The Good Woodsman*. He lives in New York City.

The Surprising Things Maui Did

by Jay Williams. Illustrated by Charles Mikolaycak.

Four Winds Press, 1979

Performing the Booktalk

Speaking Parts: Narrator One, Narrator Two, Mother, Maui, Villagers

Narrator One:	Long ago on the Hawaiian Islands, life was very different than it is now. People were cold and hungry Then a child named Maui
Maui:	was born.
Narrator One:	Because there was not enough food, Maui's mother
Mother:	sent him to live with the Sea God.
Narrator Two:	After six years Maui
Maui:	returned home
Narrator Two:	to his brothers and sisters on the islands
Maui:	and immediately life began to change.
Narrator One:	Maui played his drum
Villagers:	and birds appeared in the trees.
Narrator One:	He lifted the sky,
Villagers:	so that it lay high in the heavens.
Narrator One:	He captured the sun in a net
Maui:	and made it go more slowly, so that the land would be warm and the days longer.
Narrator Two:	But Maui spent a good deal of his time
Maui:	asleep,
Narrator Two:	and despite his wondrous deeds, he was called

The Surprising Things Maui Did

Performing the Booktalk (continued)

Villagers:	Lazy Maui!
Narrator One:	When the people of the islands decided they were tired of eating their food raw,
Villagers:	(or of climbing to the top of the volcano to cook it)
Narrator One:	they again called on Maui to help them.
Narrator Two:	And despite his laziness Maui, with the aid of a group of mud hens
Maui:	caused some *very* surprising things to happen on the islands.

Responding to the Booktalk

In groups of three or four, think of as many answers as possible to this question:

> WHAT IF Maui had refused to help the people on the islands? What would have happened?

Each group should have a secretary to write the main ideas that are given. Be prepared to share your ideas with the class.

The Surprising Things Maui Did

Book Reports

The poetry patterns on this page can be used to describe a character or scene from *The Surprising Things Maui Did.* Choose a scene or character from this or another favorite tale and use one of the patterns below to tell about it.

Five Senses Poem

Hawaiian Islands

Line
1-Color
2-Sound
3-Taste
4-Smell
5-Sight
6-Feeling

Phone Number Poem

(Tell about one of Maui's deeds)

Each line has the number of syllables in a chosen phone number

3
3
4
7
5
6
6

Adverb Poem

Tell how the people felt about Maui.

1 Adverb
2 Adverb
3 Adverb
4 Noun
5 Verb
6 Noun with description
7 Any word

Build A Name Poem

M

A

U

I

Bio Poem

Line

1 First name Maui
2 Four traits
3 Related to
4 Cares deeply about
5 Who feels
6 Who needs
7 Who gives
8 Who fears
9 Who would like to see
10 Resident of

The Surprising Things Maui Did

Products from the Hawaiin Islands

The Hawaiian Islands are well known for three crops grown there: coconuts, pineapples and coffee.

Look at the process poem below. It tells all of the steps necessary to have fresh pineapple on your breakfast table.

Find the steps necessary for your parents to have a cup of coffee or for you to enjoy a coconut candy bar. Use the pattern below to report your information.

Example:

I WONDER WHY....

THEY

Contour the fields

Plant the "suckers"

Spray and weed

Pick and load

Peel and cut

Trim and grade

Pack in cans

Ship to market

And advertise special sales on

PINEAPPLES

When I could have an apple instead!

More Picture Story Books About Hawaii

PICTURE BOOKS

Laird, Donivee Martin. *The Three Little Hawaiian Pigs and the Magic Shark*. Illustrated by Carol Jossem. Bess Press, 1981.
The Hawaiian version of "The Three Little Pigs."

McGuire-Turcotte, Casey A. *How Honu the Turtle Got His Shell*. Illustrated by Dick Sakahara. Raintree, 1990.
A Hawaiian tale of the first turtle to wear a shell.

Thompson, Vivian L. *Kawelo: Roving Chief*. Illustrated by Patricia A. Wozniak. University of Hawaii Press, 1991.
A young warrior of Kaua'i outwits and conquers his enemies.

Tune, Suelyn Ching. *How Maui Slowed the Sun*. Illustrated by Robin Yoko Burningham. University of Hawaii Press, 1988.
The tale of how Maui slows the path of the sun across the sky allowing a longer growing season for crops and children more time to play.

Tune, Suelyn Ching, Reteller. *Maui and the Secret of Fire*. Illustrated by Robin Yoko Burningham. University of Hawaii, 1991.
Maui is taught how to make fire by a mud hen.

Tune, Suelyn Ching, Reteller. *Maui Goes Fishing*. Illustrated by Robin Yoko Burningham. University of Hawaii, 1991.
Maui unearths the Hawaiian Islands with a fishing hook.

Williams, Julie Stewart. *And the Birds Appeared*. Illustrated by Robin Yoko Burningham. University of Hawaii Press, 1988.
The legend of how magical Maui makes the birds appear in Hawaii.

NON-FICTION

Aylesworth, Thomas G. *The Pacific*. Chelsea House, 1988. (Gr. 4-6)
Discusses the geographical, historical and cultural aspects of California and Hawaii.

Feeney, Stephanie. *Hawaii is a Rainbow*. Photos by Jeff Reese. University of Hawaii Press, 1985. (Gr. 3-4)
Shows things in Hawaii, including clothing, plants, insects, birds, animals, foods and flowers which are different colors of the rainbow.

Penisten, John. *Honolulu*. Dillon, 1990. (Gr. 3-4)
Describes the history, neighborhoods, attractions and festivals of Honolulu.

Stanley, Fay. *The Last Princess*. Illustrated by Diane Stanley. Four Winds, 1991.
The story of Princess Ka'iulani of Hawaii.

The Old Woman and the Red Pumpkin: A Bengali Folk Tale

Translated by Betsy Bang. Illustrated by Molly Bang.
Macmillan, 1975

Topic Talking
Primary Pre-Reading Activity

1. Assign partners.
2. State a topic.
3. Partner A talks on the topic to B until you say "Switch" (after 10 seconds)
4. Partner B talks on the same topic until you say "Stop". (10 seconds)
5. Follow the procedure with a second topic (30 seconds) and a third topic (one minute).
6. Over a period of time slowly increase the amount of time and the size of the group.

Teacher Guidelines for Topic Talking:

1. Topics should be those that students know something about.
2. Topics can be assigned and time allowed for preparation.
3. As students become comfortable with Topic Talking, increase the group size to three, then four, etc. As groups increase in size only one or two students will do topic talking for that class period.
4. As a variation of the procedure above, try this: Student A speaks to Student B on a topic for the allotted time. When you say "Switch", Student B tells Student A what he or she said until you say "Stop".
5. This activity can be used at any grade level. Topics for elementary grades should always be concrete in nature.

Topics for *The Old Woman and the Red Pumpkin*

bears
playing tricks
singing

The Old Woman and the Red Pumpkin: A Bengali Folk Tale

Booktalk

India

A bear and a tiger saw a huge red pumpkin rolling along and singing. They gave it a push and followed curiously behind it, until a jackal joined them.

"What's a pumpkin doing singing?" the Jackal said. He took a stick, broke open the pumpkin, and out popped the very same little old lady the animals had been planning to eat. But the clever old lady, who had outwitted them once before, knew just how to do it again. And she made her way safely home.

About the Author and Illustrator

Betsy Bang spent a year and a half in Calcutta and while there, learned to read Bengali. Her daughter, Molly Bang, spent half a year in Calcutta, illustrating village life. In *The Old Woman and the Red Pumpkin* we find a perfect blend of text and illustration.

Responding to the Booktalk

Work in small groups to respond to the following questions: (Each group should choose a secretary to write the main ideas of the group.)

1. Predict what the old woman will do to escape the hungry animals. Then read the rest of the story to see how the author solved the problem.
2. How many ways can your group list that *The Old Woman and The Red Pumpkin* and *The Gingerbread Man* are alike?

    A. ______________________________

    B. ______________________________

    C. ______________________________

The Old Woman and the Red Pumpkin

Performing the Booktalk

Speaking Parts: Narrator, The Tiger, The Jackal, Old Lady, The Bear

Narrator:	A bear and a tiger
Bear/Tiger:	saw a huge red pumpkin rolling along and singing.
Narrator:	They gave it a push
Bear/Tiger:	and followed curiously behind it
Narrator:	until a jackal
Jackal:	joined them. "What's a pumpkin doing singing?"
Narrator:	the jackal said. He took a stick
Jackal:	broke open the pumpkin,
Old Lady:	And out popped
Narrator:	the very same little old lady
Old Lady:	the animals had been planning to eat.
Narrator:	But the clever old lady
Old Lady:	who had outwitted them once before, knew just how to do it again.
Narrator:	And she made her way
Old Lady:	safely home.

Singing About The Old Woman and the Red Pumpkin

In the story the old woman told the animals that she would taste better if she were fatter. She then went to her daughter's house and sure enough, she ate and ate and ate, and she did get fatter.

Suppose the old woman came to your house for a meal. What would you have to eat? Name three things.

____

____

____

Look carefully at this song pattern for "Skip to My Lou." Complete the blank spaces in the pattern below with *your* favorite foods.

Sing to the tune of "Skip to My Lou"

WE LIKE:

Fried chicken sizzling in the pan
Crispy carrots chilling in a bowl
Chocolate ice cream melting in a cone
Eat, clever lady, eat!

Your Turn:

I LIKE:

____________ ____________ ____________ ____________

____________ ____________ ____________ ____________

____________ ____________ ____________ ____________

Eat, clever woman, eat!

About India

Pattern Report

See what you can discover about India. Find the capital and a large city. Now find some things that are manufactured there and some crops that are grown there. Fill in the blanks in the song below. Sing it to your class to the tune of "She'll Be Coming Around the Mountain."

Country ______________________________

Capital ______________________________

Large city ______________________________

Three manufactured goods ______________________________

____

Three crops ______________________________

Use the information to complete the "Coming Around the Mountain" song below.

She'll be coming from ______________________(Capital)
when she comes.
She'll be coming from ______________________ (Large city)
when she comes.
She'll bring __________, and __________and __________(Three products)
She'll Bring__________, and __________and __________ (Three crops)
She'll be coming from India when she comes.(Country)

More Folktales from India

PICTURE BOOKS

Demi. *The Hallowed Horse: A Folktale From India*. Illustrated by the author. Dodd Mead, 1987.
With his kingdom threatened by a snake monster, a young king searches for the rare Hallowed Horse to save his people.

Kamen, Gloria. *The Ringdoves: A Tale From India*. Illustrated by the author. Atheneum, 1988.
A mouse and a crow join forces to outwit a hunter.

Newton, Pam. *The Stonecutter: An Indian Folktale*. Illustrated by the author. Putnam's, 1990.
A stonecutter wishes for many things and discovers he is happiest being a stonecutter.

Rose, Deborah Lee. *The People Who Hugged the Trees: An Environmental Folktale*. Illustrated by Birgitta Saflune. Roberts Rinehart, 1990.
A legend from India telling how the people of a village protect their trees.

White, Rosalyn. *The Power of a Promise*. Illustrated by the author. Dharma, 1989.
The story of the efforts of a truthful prince to reform a terrible monster.

NON-FICTION

Cumming, David. *India*. Photographs by Jimmy Holmes. Illustrated by Peter Bull. Bookwright Press 1989. (Gr. 3-4)
Discusses India's history, culture, geography and economy.

India in Pictures. Prepared by the Geography Department of Lerner Publications. 1989. (Gr. 4-6)
Geography, history, government, society and economics of this diverse country.

Inside India. by Prodeepta Das. Photographs by Prodeepta Das, Franklin Watts, 1990.
This book gives basic information about India including, the land, family life. food, sports, history and farming.

Fin M'Coul and the Giant: From Celtic Fairy Tales
by Joseph Jacobs
Blue Ribbon Books, 1899

Booktalk

Ireland

Fin M'Coul, the legendary giant of Ireland and Scotland, was working one day on the causeway to make a bridge across to Scotland when word came that the giant, Cuhullin, was coming to challenge Fin to a fight. Now everyone knows that Cuhullin can smash thunderbolts, pick up houses and use trees for walking sticks. Fin was worried, so he headed home to ask his wife, Oonagh, what could be done? Oonagh dressed Fin in baby clothes and baked cakes with an iron griddle in the center of each. When Cuhullin arrived she told him that Fin was not home and asked if he would like to sit a spell and have some cakes. The cake with the iron center was given to Cuhullin. A different cake was given to the "baby." When Cuhullin broke a tooth but saw the baby happily eating, he had second thoughts about challenging Fin to a fight. "If the child is stronger than I, what must the father be like?" he thought. And Cuhullin was never heard from again!

Other tales about Fin M'Coul can be found in: *The High Deeds of Finn Mac Cool* by Rosemary Sutcliff. E.P. Dutton, 1967.

A delightful picture book version is: *Fin M'Coul: The Giant of Knockmany Hill* written and illustrated by Tomie DePaola. Holiday House, 1981.

Finn MacCool and the Men of Small Deeds by Pat O'Shea. Illustrated by Stephen Lavis. Oxford University Press, 1987.

Fin M'Coul and the Giant: From Celtic Fairy Tales

by Joseph Jacobs

Blue Ribbon Books, 1899

Performing the Booktalk

Speaking Parts: Narrator One, Narrator Two, Fin M'Coul, Culhullin, Oonagh

Narrator One:	Fin M'Coul, the legendary giant of Ireland and Scotland
Fin:	was working one day on the causeway to make a bridge across to Scotland
Narrator Two:	when word came that the giant, Cuhullin,
Cuhullin:	was coming to challenge Fin to a fight.
Narrator Two:	Now everyone knows that Cuhullin can
Cuhullin:	smash thunderbolts, pick up houses and use trees for walking sticks.
Narrator One:	Fin was worried so he
Fin:	headed home
Narrator Two:	to ask his wife, Oonagh
Fin:	what could be done?
Narrator Two:	Oonagh
Oonagh:	dressed Fin in baby clothes and baked cakes with an iron griddle in the center of each.
Narrator One:	When Cuhullin arrived she told him that
Oonagh:	Fin was not home
Narrator One:	and asked if he would
Oonagh:	like to sit a spell and have some cakes.
Narrator Two:	The cake with the iron center was given to Cuhullin.
Narrator One:	A different cake was given to the "baby."

Performing the Booktalk (continued)

Narrator Two: When Cuhullin
Cuhullin: broke a tooth
Narrator Two: but saw the baby happily eating, he had
Cuhullin: second thoughts about challenging Fin to a fight. "If the child is stronger than I, what must the father be like?"
Narrator Two: he thought.
Fin/Oonagh: And Cuhullin was never heard from again!

Talking About The Story

Have a contest! Work in groups of four or five. Each group must have a secretary or recorder to write the main ideas of the group.

In five minutes, how many ways can your group list that *Fin M'Coul and the Giant* and *Jack and the Beanstalk* are alike?

1. ______________________________
2. ______________________________
3. ______________________________
4. ______________________________
5. ______________________________
6. ______________________________
7. ______________________________
8. ______________________________
9. ______________________________
10. ______________________________

More?????????

The winning group is the group with the longest list.

Fin M'Coul and the Giant: From Celtic Fairy Tales
Teacher Planning Page
Critical Thinking

Discuss orally after reading aloud *Fin M'Coul and the Giant.*

Fluency: The ability to make many responses. Name as many giant things as you can.

Flexibility: Finding new categories. Stretching the mind beyond the expected response.
How can you group the items you named under fluency?
What other ways might Finn have escaped his enemy instead of dressing as a baby?

Originality: Responding in new or original ways.
What group and/or items did you name that no one else named? What things did you think of (under FLEXIBILITY) that no one else thought of?

Elaboration: Adding details to make a product more complete.
Take an everyday item (pencil, toothbrush, shoe, etc). Add something to the item to make it easier or more enjoyable for a giant to use.

Planning: Determining a task to be done, the steps to take, materials needed and possible problems.
Plan a reading corner in your room for books about giants. Where will it be located? How will the books be displayed? What books will be displayed? How will students be able to read the books? How will they return them? What problems might you anticipate with the reading corner? How can each be solved?

Forecasting: Determining cause and effect. Complete these sentences:
Because Fin's enemy was coming, ______________________________

____

When Cuhullin saw how strong the baby was

____

Critical Thinking continued

Decision Making and Problem Solving
A. Examine the facts
B. State the problem
C. List alternatives
D. List criteria for judging alternatives
E. Score alternatives on a decision grid
F. State the solution

Problem
How else might Fin escape his enemy?

Fin is afraid of Cuhullin, the mean giant. He thinks Cuhullin is the stronger of the two and wants to avoid seeing him. On the lines below list ways Fin might be able to avoid a confrontation with Culhullin. Score each way to determine the best course of action for Fin. The first one is done for you. Score each idea l=no 2=maybe 3=yes.

Alternatives **Criteria**

Score 1=no, 2=maybe, 3=yes	Is it fast?	Will it work?	Easy to do?	Low cost?	Non-violent?	Total
Lock the door	**3**	**1**	**3**	**3**	**2**	**12**

Evaluation: Judging the pros and cons of an item or situation.

Finding Out About Ireland

Working with a partner or small group, decide whether each of the statements below is true or false. *Guess* if you do not know. Then read the selection (turned upside down) below to support or deny your guesses.

1. Ireland is a large city. __________
2. Ireland borders the United States. __________
3. The basis of Ireland's economy is agriculture. __________
4. The Irish grow abundant supplies of vegetables. __________
5. The land in Ireland is mostly mountainous. __________
6. The first and official language of Ireland is Irish. __________

Ireland is a nation that lies in the greater part of a unique and beautiful island west of Great Britain. These two areas are separated by the Irish Sea. Ireland consists of majestic scenery and the nation has a strong and rich culture and tradition. It is surrounded by deep and beautiful bodies of water as much of its land is flat and green. There are low hills among this flatness and there is also a mountain range on its coast. Irish is the national language and is considered its first official language. Agriculture is the basis of the economy in Ireland and Ireland's greatest asset is its climate which allows for production of many types of vegetables. Many tourists visit this beautiful country each year.

More Irish Tales

PICTURE BOOKS

Balian, Lorna. *Leprechauns Never Lie.* Illustrated by the author. Abingdon, 1980.
Ninny Nanny is lazy but discovers one has to work for a pot of gold.

Calhoun, Mary. *The Hungry Leprechaun.* Illustrated by Roger Duvoisin. HarperCollins, 1962.
An Irish fable of how the potato came to Ireland.

Cooper, Susan. *The Selkie Girl.* Illustrated by Warwick Hutton. Atheneum, 1986.
The classic tale of the girl who belongs to the sea.

Cormack, M. Grant. *Animal Tales From Ireland.* Illustrated by Vana Earle. John Day, 1955.
A collection of tales on a variety of animals.

Haugaard, Erik. *Prince Boghole.* Illustrated by Julie Downing. Macmillan, 1987.
A princess must choose from wealthy and haughty suitors or a prince from a poor kingdom.

McDermott, Gerald. *Daniel O'Rourke: An Irish Tale.* Illustrated by the author. Viking, 1986.
An adventure begins when Daniel falls asleep under a magical pooka tower.

O'Shea, Pat and Stephen Lavis. *Finn MacCool and the Small Men of Deeds.* Holiday House, 1987.
Finn MacCool tries to help a giant rescue his children.

NON-FICTION

Fairclough, Chris. *We Live in Ireland.* Bookwright Press, 1986. (Gr. 4-6)
First person interviews with residents of Ireland.

Jacobson, Peter Otto and Preben Sejer Kristensen. *A Family in Ireland.* Bookwright Press, 1985. (Gr. 3-4)
A view of an Irish home in the small village of Ballyduff and a family with three children.

James, Ian and Henry Pluckrose. *Ireland.* Franklin Watts, 1983. (Gr. 4-6)
Many facts about Ireland including size, population, major religions and largest cities.

Moran, Tom. *A Family in Ireland.* Lerner, 1986. (Gr. 3-4)
A view of life of a farm family in a small village in Ireland.

The Bell of Atri: An Old Italian Tale

found in:
***Favorite Tales of Long Ago* by James Baldwin,**
illustrated by Lili Reth, Aladdin, 1955.
***Myths and Legends of Many Lands* by Nicola Ann Sissons,**
illustrated by Robert Todd, Hart, 1962

The Story

Italy

In the mountains of Italy is a small village and in the village there is a magnificent bell. Now the villagers usually get along with each other quite well, but should a wrong be done, the person who has been wronged has merely to ring the bell. Hearing the bell the villagers all gather around to listen and to decide what can be done to right the wrong. After many years the rope on the bell rotted away and the villagers sent away for a very long rope. It must be long enough for the smallest person to reach. Until the long rope arrived, a long vine was cut and attached to the bell.

Now just outside the village lived a mean man. His faithful donkey who had worked hard and served him for many years was his only companion. But the donkey was old and could no longer work so the man beat him and chased him away. As the donkey wandered into the town what did he find but a delicious vine waiting to be eaten. As the donkey nibbled the vine the bell began to ring. "The donkey has been wronged," the villagers cried, seeing how old and thin the poor beast was. "The wrong must be righted!" And the mean man was brought to town and ordered to put aside half of his gold for the care of the donkey who, for the rest of its days had a warm stall and plenty to eat.

The Bell of Atri

Performing the Story

Speaking Parts: Narrator One, Narrator Two, Villagers (as many as desired), The Donkey, The Mean Man

Narrator One: In the mountains of Italy is a small village

Narrator Two: and in the village there is a magnificent bell. Now the villagers usually

Villagers: get along with each other quite well,

Narrator Two: but should a wrong be done, the person

Villagers: who has been wronged has merely to ring the bell.

Narrator One: Hearing the bell, the villagers

Villagers: all gather around to listen and to decide what can be done to right the wrong.

Narrator Two: After many years, the rope on the bell rotted away and the villagers

Villagers: sent away for a very long rope.

Narrator One: It must be long enough for the smallest person to reach.

Narrator Two: Until the long rope arrived, a long vine was cut and attached to the bell.

Narrator One: Now just outside the village lived

Mean Man: a mean man.

Narrator Two: His faithful donkey

Donkey: who had worked hard and served him for many years (hee haw)

Narrator Two: was his only companion. But the donkey

Donkey: was old and could no longer work

Narrator One: so the man

Mean Man: beat him and chased him away.

The Bell of Atri
Performing the Story (continued)

Narrator Two:	As the donkey
Donkey:	wandered into town (clippity clop)
Narrator Two:	what did he find but
Donkey:	a delicious vine waiting to be eaten.
Narrator Two:	As the donkey nibbled the vine the bell began to ring.
Villagers:	"The donkey has been wronged!"
Narrator One:	the villagers cried, seeing how old and thin the poor beast was.
Villagers:	"The wrong must be righted!"
Narrator One:	And the mean man
Mean Man:	was brought to town and ordered
Villagers:	to put aside half of his gold for the care of the donkey
Narrator Two:	who, for the rest of his days
Donkey:	had a warm stall and plenty to eat.

Responding to the Story

In small groups of three or four find as many ways as you can that this story (*The Bell of Atri*) is like the story of *Cinderella*. One person in your group can list the ideas of the group. Can your group think of at least five ways the two stories are alike? More than five?

1. ______________________________
2. ______________________________
3. ______________________________
4. ______________________________
5. ______________________________

The Bell of Atri

Cause and Effect

Because...

The donkey was old and could no longer work ...

What happened was...

The mean man beat him and chased him away.

Complete the following

1. **Because** the rope on the village bell broke
   What happened was ______________________________

   ____

2. **Because** the donkey was hungry when he came into the village
   What happened was ______________________________

   ____

3. **Because** the villagers saw the starving donkey ringing the bell
   What happened was ______________________________

   ____

The Bell of Atri: Recalling the Story

The "I Have, Who Has" Game

To play the game you will need five players. Cut the cards apart and mix them up. Each player gets one card. The player with the stars on his/her card(**) begins by reading the "WHO HAS" part of the card. The player with the correct answer reads the "I HAVE" part of his/her card and then reads the WHO HAS portion. The game continues until all cards are read and the story is told.

I Have:	The villagers forced the mean master to give gold for the donkey's care.
** Start here:	
Who Has:	Why did the village need a bell?

I Have:	The village needed a bell to ring when a wrong had been done.
Who Has:	What happened when the bell was rung?

I Have:	The villagers would gather and try to right the wrong.
Who Has:	Why was the bell rope made from a vine?

I Have:	The rope was made from a vine when the long rope broke.
Who Has:	Who pulled on the vine rope and what happened?

I Have:	The donkey pulled on the vine rope and the villagers saw how thin he was.
Who Has:	How did the villagers right the wrong that had been done to the donkey?

About Italy

Italy is a country in southern Europe. It is shaped like a boot and is noted for its beautiful scenery and very old buildings. Italy has many high mountains and no place in the "boot" is more than 65 miles from the sea. The people love art and music and good food. In the mountains they raise sheep and goats, olives and grapes. If you visited Italy you could go to an opera and hear beautiful music, or visit one of the many art museums. You could ride in a gondola on the Grand Canal of Venice or climb the Alps, one of the most famous mountain chains in the world.

TAKE A POLL!!! Ask eight different classmates which one of the things listed below they would like to do if they visited Italy.

Students surveyed	Go to an opera	Visit a museum	Ride in a gondola	Climb a mountain
A				
B				
C				
D				
E				
F				
G				
H				

The activity with the most choices is ______________________________

____

The second most popular activity would be _________________________

____

Picture Story Books Set in Italy

PICTURE BOOKS

Basile, Giambattista. *Petrosinella*. Illustrated by Diane Stanley. Waren, 1981.
Petrosinella (the Italian Rapunzel) breaks the enchantment put on her by an ogress who keeps her prisoner with the aid of three acorns.

Cauley, Lorinda Bryan. *The Goose and the Golden Coins*. Illustrated by the author. Harcourt, 1981.
Two sisters named Lilla and Lolla take pity on a goose who repays them by dropping coins.

Cazzona, Gus. *The Bells of Santa Lucia*. Illustrated by Pierr Morgan. Philomel, 1991.
Lucinda does not want to hear bells after the death of her grandmother. But a fire that threatens small animals shows her that the bells are not to be feared.

Cossi, Olga. *Orlanda and the Contest of Thieves*. Illustrated by Tom Sarmo. Bookmakers, 1989.
A tale about a girl who proves she is the greatest thief in the world.

dePaola, Tomie. *Strega Nona*. Illustrated by the author. Prentice-Hall, 1975.
Big Anthony, Strega Nona's helper, tries out a spell on the pasta pot that has disastrous results.

dePaola, Tomie. *Tony's Bread: An Italian Folktale*. Illustrated by the author. Whitebird, 1989.
A tale about the origin of panettone.

Haviland, Virginia. *Favorite Fairy Tales Told in Italy*. Illustrated by Evaline Ness. Little-Brown, 1965.
A variety of short, easy-to-read tales from Italy.

Lager, Claude. *A Tale of Two Rats*. Illustrated by Nicole Rutten. Stewart, 1991.
An artist, Arthur, finds success in selling his paintings in Italy but finds he must make a difficult choice and that fame is not everything.

Manson, Christopher. *The Crab Prince: An Entertainment for Children*. Illustrated by the author. Holt, 1991.
A young girl rescues a prince who has been turned into a crab by an evil enchantress.

Nones, Eric Jon. *The Canary Prince*. Illustrated by the author. Farrar, 1991.
A tale of a prince and princess, a stepmother and a magic charm.

NON-FICTION

Haskins, Jim. *Count Your Way Through Italy*. Illustrated by Beth Wright. Carolrhoda Books, 1990.
This book uses the numbers one through ten in Italian to introduce the country and culture of Italy.

Powell, Jillian. *Italy*. Illustrated by Peter Bull. Photographs by Julia Davey. Bookwright Press, 1990.
Two page spreads and color photographs describe the climate, sports, food, and living conditions in Italy today.

The Tongue-Cut Sparrow

retold by Lafcadio Hearn

***Japanese Fairy Tales*, Liveright, 1924.**

also found in *Favorite Fairy Tales Told in Japan* by Virginia Haviland. Little Brown, 1962

Booktalk

Japan

Long ago there was an old woman who was cranky and mean. One morning she had mixed starch for her clothes when a small sparrow flew down and ate it all. The mean old woman cut out the sparrow's tongue and the bird flew away. Now the bird had been the neighbors' pet and the unhappy neighbors set off to find it. Deep in the forest they found the small bird's new home. They were welcomed and fed and given the choice of a heavy or light basket to take home. Since the neighbor couple was old, they chose the lightest basket. When they arrived home they found the basket filled with riches. Now the cranky old woman heard about this and set off the to find the sparrow. Do you suppose she will come home with a basket of riches? To find out, read *The Tongue-Cut Sparrow*.

About the Collector

Lafcadio Hearn was a Greek— Irish American who treasured Japanese stories and culture. Mr. Hearn made a life's work of collecting tales that might otherwise have been forgotten and retelling them for Americans.

About Japan

Four large islands and many smaller ones that stretch for 1250 miles make up the country of Japan. It lies in the Pacific Ocean along the eastern coast of Asia. Many goods are produced in Japan and shipped to other parts of the world. Japanese artists are famous for their delicate paintings and wood block prints.

The Tongue-Cut Sparrow
retold by Lafcadio Hearn

Performing the Booktalk

Speaking Parts: Narrator One, Narrator Two, Old Woman, Two Neighbors, Sparrow

Narrator One: Long ago there was an old woman who was

Old Woman: cranky and mean.

Narrator One: One morning she had mixed starch for her clothes when a small sparrow

Sparrow: flew down and ate it all (peep! peep!)

Narrator One: The mean old woman

Old Woman: cut out the sparrow's tongue

Narrator Two: and the sparrow

Sparrow: flew away. (Peep! Peep!)

Narrator Two: Now the bird had been the neighbors' pet and the unhappy neighbors

Neighbors: set off to find it.

Narrator Two: Deep in the forest they found

Neighbors: the small bird's new home.

Narrator One: They were welcomed and fed and

Sparrow: given the choice of a heavy or light basket to take home.

Narrator Two: Since the neighbor couple was old, they

Neighbors: chose the lightest basket.

The Tongue-Cut Sparrow
Performing the Booktalk (continued)

Narrator Two:	When they arrived home they found the basket
Neighbors:	filled with riches.
Narrator One:	Now the cranky old woman
Old Woman:	heard about this and set off to find the sparrow.
Narrator Two:	Do you suppose she will come home
Old Woman:	with a basket of riches?
Narrator One:	To find out read
All:	*The Tongue-Cut Sparrow.*

Retelling the Story in Verse

A mean old woman took a tiny bird,
And cut its tongue so it couldn't be heard.
The bird flew away and the neighbors gave chase,
And followed the bird to a tree-filled place.

They were welcomed and fed and before they could ask it,
Were given a marvelous, magical basket.

The mean old woman, she wanted one, too.
So went to find the bird to see what it would do.
"Give me jewels," she said, "and a fancy dress."
Did the bird give her jewels? What would you guess?

Now the neighbors were gentle and kind and needy,
But the cranky old woman was mean and greedy.
So her gift wasn't silver or jewels or gold
But a basket of troubles, now the story's told.

Learning About Japan

Working with a partner or small group, decide on the best answer to each of the following questions. *Guess* if you do not know. Then listen to or read the article about Japan on the next page to support or deny your guesses.

1. What is the name of a Japanese utensil used for eating?

   A) bamboo B) pogo C) chopsticks

2. A house made of "shoji" would be made of

   A) brick B) wood C) paper

3. A good pet in Japan would be a

   A) horse B) dog C) cricket

4. A Bonsi is a

   A) small tree B) flower C) fish

5. A kimono is a

   A) doll B) dress C) house

6. A favorite Japanese food is

   A) potatoes B) rice C) carrots

7. What type of money is used in Japan?

   A) Yen B) Frank C) dollar

8. Which meat is often eaten raw?

   A) pork B) fish C) beef

Answers: 1.C 2.C 3.C 4.A 5.B 6.B 7.A 8.B

About Japan

Boys and girls in Japan enjoy many of the same activities as boys and girls in the United States. They like to play baseball, go to the beach for picnics and watch television. They eat with a spoon and with chopsticks and especially like rice and raw fish. They usually can't have a puppy in the house because it would tear the shoji or paper doors or dig up the tiny Bonsi trees. A Japanese child who had saved enough yen to buy a pet might buy a cricket and cricket cage or a goldfish. On special occasions the girls wear dresses called kimonos.

Use one or more of the facts in the paragraph above to write a COMPARE/CONTRAST poem about Japan and the United States.

EXAMPLE

If I lived in JAPAN
I would grow rice
And eat with chopsticks
But I wouldn't spend dollars
Because people in the United States do that.

YOUR TURN

If I lived in ______________________________
I would ______________________________
And ______________________________
But I wouldn't______________________________
Because people in the United States do that.

More Books About Japan

PICTURE BOOKS

Friedman, Ina R. and Say, Allen. *How My Parents Learned to Eat*. Houghton Mifflin Company, 1984.
A Japanese lady falls in love with an American soldier and they learn to eat with both forks and chopsticks.

Hodges, Margaret. *The Wave.*Illustrated by Blair Lent. Houghton Mifflin Co., 1964.
An old man sacrifices his rice fields in order to warn the villagers that a tidal wave is coming.

Kalman, Maira. *Sayonare, Mrs. Kackleman.* Viking Kestrel, Penguin Group, 1989.
This book tells about a visit to Japan and the sights that tourists will see.

Morimoto, Junko. *The Inch Boy*. Illustrated by the author. Viking Penguin Inc., 1984.
An old couple finds a one inch boy on their steps. He never grows but wants to be a Samurai warrior. He goes off to prove himself and after injuring a big bad giant he takes the giant's magic hammer and becomes a tall man.

Sakai, Kimiko and Arai, Tomie. *Sachiko Means Happiness*. Children's Book Press, 1990.
This book tells about a Grandmother and her Granddaughter, who was given the same name as her Grandmother.

Wisniewski, David. *The Warrior and the Wise Man.* Illustrated by the author. William Morrow, 1989.
The Emperor has twin sons and can not decide who shall inherit the throne. The sons set out in quest of five eternal elements. One son uses his strength and the other uses his wisdom to gain these elements.

Yagwa, Sumiko. *The Crane Wife*. Illustrated by Suekichi Akaba. Morrow, 1981.
Yohei removes an arrow from a wounded crane. A beautiful woman appears and offers to marry Yohei and weave cloth to help feed them. Yohei becomes greedy and wants more cloth. After being warned never to watch the weaving, Yohei discovers the crane.

NON-FICTION

Davis, James E. *Tokyo* Raintree Publishers, 1990.
This book describes homes, schools, industry, religion, festivals, historical events, points of interests, and customs in and around the capitol city of Tokyo.

James, Ian. *Inside Japan*. Franklin Watts, 1989.
This book tells about the land, the people and their history, the towns and cities, family life, food, sports and pastimes, and the various other facts about Japan.

Gonyo and the Princess: A Mexican Tale

by Verna Aardema

Found in *Best Ever Writing Models*, Book Lures, 1991

Booktalk

Mexico

Gonyo Gonzales lived in the palace of the king. When the king heard about a princess with golden hair he sent Gonyo to find her. The journey was a long one, but with the help of a fly, a dove and a small fish, Gonyo finds the princess and takes her to the king. The princess is dismayed to find that the king is very old and insists that she will not marry him until he sends someone to fetch water from the Spring of Life. Again Gonyo sets out and once again he is successful. Before trying the water himself the king orders Gonyo to be put to death, then sprinkled with the water to see if it will bring him back to life. Gonyo dies and the princess steps forth to sprinkle the water from a small pearl bottle. Will the water bring him back to life? If it does will the princess have to keep her promise and marry the king? It is Gonyo she truly loves. To find out, read one of the many versions of this old, old tale.

Other versions are:

"The Water of Life" found in *Grimm's Fairy Tales*. Illustrated by Jiri Trnks. Paul Hamlyn, 1961

The Water of Life Retold by Barbara Rogasky. Illustrated by Trina Schart Hyman. Holiday House, 1986.

These two versions are of German origin and vary in many ways from the Mexican version above. Students will enjoy finding the similarities and differences.

About the Author

Verna Aardema began her writing career at the age of eleven with encouragement from her mother who believed that being a writer was a very fine thing! She took time out from her writing to become a teacher, a wife and a mother. Her interest in tales from other countries led to her searching for little known stories and giving them new "garments" to be enjoyed by children today.

Gonyo and the Princess: A Mexican Tale

by Verna Aardema

Found in *Best Ever Writing Models*, Book Lures, 1991

Performing the Booktalk

Speaking Parts: Narrator One, Narrator Two, Gonyo, King, Princess

Narrator One:	Gonyo Gonzales
Gonyo:	lived in the palace of the king.
Narrator Two:	When the king heard about
King:	a princess with golden hair,
Narrator Two:	he sent Gonyo to find her.
Narrator One:	The journey was a long one but with the help of a fly, a dove and a small fish, Gonyo
Gonyo:	finds the princess and takes her to the king.
Narrator Two:	The princess
Princess:	is dismayed to find that the king is very old
Narrator Two:	and insists she will not marry him until he
Princess:	sends someone to fetch water from the Spring of Life.
Narrator One:	Again Gonyo
Gonyo:	sets out
Narrator One:	and once again he
Gonyo:	is successful.
Narrator Two:	Before trying the water himself, the king
King:	orders Gonyo to be put to death, then sprinkled with the water to see if it will bring him back to life.
Narrator One:	Gonyo dies and the princess
Princess:	steps forth to sprinkle the water from a small pearl bottle.
Narrator One:	Will the water bring him back to life?
Narrator Two:	If it does, will the princess have to keep her promise and
Princess:	marry the king?

Performing the Booktalk (continued)

Narrator Two:	It is Gonyo she
Princess:	truly loves.
Both Narrators:	To find out, read one of the many versions of this old, old tale.

About Mexico

Mexico is a beautiful country with high mountains, vast deserts and sea shore villages. The people celebrate many fiestas or parties which include Mexican food (tortillas, tacos). A festive Mexican dance performed at many fiestas is the Mexican Hat Dance. The people dress in brightly colored clothes and sombreros. Treasures of gold, silver and jewels are an interesting part of the history of Mexico. The Mexican people value their history and ancient culture. The arts and crafts such as silversmithing, pottery and weaving are still done in much the way they were done hundreds of year ago. A Sunday afternoon outing at the bullfights can be very exciting.

Use Information from the paragraph above to write an "If I visited Mexico" paragraph. Use the format below.

If I visited Mexico
I could attend a fiesta
Dress in bright clothes
And wear a sombrero
But I couldn't catch salmon or climb Denali
Because people from Alaska do that.

If I visited Mexico
I could ____________________
And ____________________
And ____________________
But I couldn't ____________________
____
Because people from
____________________ do that.

A Writing Activity

Suppose that Gonyo, who fell in love with the princess decided not to take her to the king. Pretend that you are Gonyo and you have arrived at the palace alone to explain to the king why the princess is not with you.

Look at the items below. Use at least three in your excuse to the king to explain why you did not bring the princess to be his bride.

ball of string	a stray cat	a deserted hacienda
firecrackers	a corn field	the village well
an escaped animal	an old man	a cross-eyed woman
a pitcher of water		

To The King of All the Haciendas:
The reason that I was not able to bring the princess back to the palace was ____

____

____

____

____

____

____

____

____

____

____

____

____

Signed *Gonyo*

Your Name ______________________________________

Write a Five Senses Poem

In *Gonyo and the Princess*, Gonyo had to travel all through Mexico to find the princess. He walked across deserts, he climbed mountains and he crossed rivers and lakes to make his way to the seacoast.

Choose one of these: mountain, river, lake, desert. Write a five senses poem about it. See the example below about the seacoast.

The Seacoast

The seacoast is a blue-green mist.
It sounds like waves in the wind.
It tastes salty on the tongue.
It smells like a fish market.
It looks like it goes on forever.
It makes me feel like taking off my shoes and running in the sand.

Five Senses Poem

Line
1-Color ____________________
2-Sound ____________________
3-Taste ____________________
4-Smell ____________________
5-Sight ____________________
6-Feeling ____________________

More Picture Story Books About Mexico

PICTURE BOOKS

Aardema, Verna. *Borreguita and the Coyote: A Tale From Ayutla, Mexico*. Illustrated by Petra Mathers. Knopf, 1991.
A small lamb named Borreguita is pursued by a coyote but manages to escape.

Aardema, Verna. *Pedro and the Padre: A Tale From Jalisco, Mexico*. Illustrated by Frisco Henstra. Dial, 1991.
Lazy Pedro almost drowns because of one of his lies and learns to change his ways.

Ets, Marie Hall and Aurora Labastida. *Nine Days to Christmas*. Illustrated by Marie Hall Ets. Charles Scribner's Sons, 1949.
Ceci' is now old enough to have her own posada (a party given for the nine days before Christmas) but must wait patiently for the days to arrive.

Sonneborn, Ruth. *Friday Night is Papa Night*. Illustrated by Emily McCully. Viking Press, 1970.
Pedro and his family are cleaning the house for their father's one night home only to be filled with anxiety when papa does not arrive until long after supper and bedtime.

Taha, Karen. *A Gift for Tia*. Illustrated by Dee deRosa. Dillon Press, 1986.
Carmela was sad because she had never given anything to Tia Rosa while the old woman lived, then finishes a blanket for Tia Rose's granddaughter.

Tompert, Ann. *The Silver Whistle*. Illustrated by Beth Peck. Macmillan, 1988.
Miguel worked hard to buy a silver whistle but first bought a mule and traded it for a serape. He then gave the serape to a cold, little boy but was left with only an odd shaped bird as an offering to the holy infant.

NON-FICTION

Jacobson, Karen. *Mexico*. Photographs by Lila Podendorf. Children's Press, 1982.
An introduction to the land, people, homes and customs of Mexico for beginning readers.

Moran, Tom. *A Family in Mexico*. Lerner Publications, 1987.
A brief introduction to a typical town in Mexico showing the town square, homes, jobs and schools.

Reilly, Mary Jo. *Mexico*. Cavindish, 1991.
A good reference book for questions that may arise during a study of Mexico.

Why Flies Buzz
from *African Myths and Legends*
by Kathleen Arnott

Henry Z. Walck, Inc. 1962

Booktalk

Africa

This tale begins when an old man in a tree is bothered by a fly. The man drops his knife and frightens a snake who slithers into a rat's hole. The rat runs up a tree, scaring a monkey who drops a mango in the bush fowl's nest, breaking all the eggs. The bush fowl is so unhappy that she will no longer call the sun to rise each morning and the world becomes dark. Of course, the other jungle animals are not a bit pleased with this state of affairs and take their problem to the Great Spirit. What do you suppose the Great Spirit does when the fly is revealed as the cause of all the problems? Read *Why Flies Buzz* or read the modern picture book version of this old, old tale, *Why Mosquitoes Buzz in People's Ears* by Verna Aardema. Illustrated by Leo Dillon. Dial Books, 1975.

Performing the Booktalk

Speaking Parts: Old Man, Snake, Rat, Monkey, Other Animals, Narrator

Narrator: This tale begins when an old man in a tree

Old Man: is bothered by a fly.

Narrator: The man drops his knife

Old Man: and frightens a snake who

Snake: slithers into a rat's hole.

Narrator: The rat

Rat: runs up a tree, scaring a monkey who

Monkey: drops a mango in the bush fowl's nest, breaking all the eggs.

Narrator: The bush fowl is so unhappy that she

Bush Fowl: will no longer call the sun each morning

Why Flies Buzz

Performing the Booktalk (continued)

Narrator: and the world becomes dark. Of course, the other jungle animals
Animals: are not a bit pleased with this state of affairs
Narrator: and take their problem
Animals: to the Great Spirit.
Narrator: What do you suppose the Great Spirit does when the fly is revealed
Animals: as the cause of all the problems? To find out, read *Why Flies Buzz.*

Which One?

There are many animals found in the jungles and grasslands of Africa. This tale mentioned the snake, the rat, the monkey and the bush fowl. All of these animals *except one* might have gone to the Great Spirit to complain about the dark world. Can you discover which one of these is *not* an African animal?

crocodile
tiger
hippo
elephant

lion
giraffe
rhino
rabbit

Answer: The tiger is an Asian animal, not African.

Why Flies Buzz

The "I Have, Who Has" Game

Cut apart the story strips below. The student with card #1 reads the "Who Has" part of the card. The student holding the card with the answer reads the "I Have" part of the card and then reads the "Who Has" question. The game continues until all cards are read.

I Have:	The bush fowl refused to call the sun each day.
Who Has:	What did fly do to the old man?

I Have:	Fly caused the old man to drop his knife, scaring a snake who slithered down a rat hole.
Who Has:	What did rat do?

I Have:	Rat ran up a tree scaring monkey.
Who Has:	What did monkey do?

I Have:	Monkey dropped a mango in bush fowl's nest, breaking all of her eggs.
Who Has:	How did bush fowl feel when her eggs were broken.

I Have:	Bush fowl was very sad when her eggs were broken.
Who Has:	What did bush fowl refuse to do?

Jungle Animals
A Beginning Research Activity

Choose one African animal. Find information about the animal in the encyclopedia and create a data bank.

Here is a data bank about the python.

Data Bank - Python

Lives	Eats	What It Does
Asia	small animals	climbs
Africa	rabbits	swims
India	wild pigs	swallows prey whole
tropical forests		winds around a prey
low dense growth		squeezes
		hatches from eggs

Looks Like	Has
20-30 feet long	up to 100 eggs at a time
tough skin	
bold pattern	
very large	

Your Data Bank - ________________(animal)

Lives	Eats	What It Does

Looks Like	Has

Use the information in your Data Bank to write a song about the animal

Example:
(Tune: London Bridge)

Pythons can be 30 feet long
30 feet long
30 feet long
Pythons can be 30 feet long
And live in Africa.

(Tune: Did You Ever See a Lassie)

Did you ever see a python
A python
A python
Did you ever see a python
Climb trees in the forest?

Your turn:

Did you ever see a ____________________
A ______________________________
A ______________________________
Did you ever see a ____________________
____

More Tales from Africa

PICTURE BOOKS

Aardema, Verna. *Bimwili and the Zimwwi: A Tale from Zanzibar*, retold by Verna Aardema. Illustrated by Susan Meddaugh. Dial, 1985.
Bimwili finds a magic shell that causes her to fall into the hands of Zimwwi. She must get free.

Aardema, Verna. *Bringing the Rain to Kapiti Plain; A Nandi Tale* retold by Verna Aardema. Illustrated by Beatriz Vidal. Dial, 1981.
This story tells about the dry plains of Kapiti and of the boy, Ki-Pat, who finds a way to make the dark cloud release the rain.

Aardema, Verna. *Half-a-Ball-of-Kenki.* Illustrated by Diane Stanley Zuromskis. Warne, 1979.
This tale explains how the leopard gets its spots, and its comeuppance.

Aardema, Verna. *Oh Kojo! How Could You!* retold by Verna Aardema. Illustrated by Marc Brown. Dial, 1984.
Ananse always tricks Kojo out of his money, until the cat helps out.

Aardema, Verna. *Vingananee and the Tree Toad: A Liberian Tale*, retold by Verna Aardema. Illustrated by Ellen Weiss. Warne, 1983.
The rat, the buck deer and lion fail to guard their home against the Vingananee, but the small tree toad succeeds.

Aardema, Verna. *What's So Funny, Ketu? A Neur Tale*. Illustrated by Marc Brown, Dial, 1982.
Ketu saves a snake and in return the snake gives him the ability to understand animals.

Aardema, Verna. *Who's in Rabbit's House? A Masai Tale.* Illustrated Leo Dillon and Diane Dillon. Dial, 1977.
A play about a rabbit who can't get into her house, because Long One is inside and is threatening her. Rabbit unexpectedly solves the problem.

NON-FICTION

Chiasson, John C. *African Journey*. Bradbury Press, 1987. (Gr. 4-8)
The culture and daily life of people in six regions of Africa.

Griffin, Michael. *A Family in Kenya*. Photos by Liba Taylor. Lerner, 1988. (Gr. 4-6)
Describes the home, school, work customs and day-to-day life of a girl living with her family in Kenya.

Musgrove, Margaret. *Ashanti to Zulu: African Traditions*. Illustrated by Leo and Diane Dillon. Dial, 1976.
An introduction to twenty-six African peoples with information about the customs of each.

The Maid on the Glass Mountain

from *East O the Sun and West O the Moon*

by Peter Asbjornsen

Putnam's, 1908

Picture Book versions include: *Boots and the Glass Mountain* by Claire Martin. Illustrated by Gennady Spirin. Dial Books, 1992

Booktalk

Norway

It is midnight on St. John's night and Cinderlad is crouched in the hayloft waiting to see what strange creature comes on this special night each year to eat all of the grass in the meadow. The two previous years his brothers had been sent to watch but were so frightened by the clatter and the noise that they ran away. A rumble in the distance grew louder and louder. The hayloft shook and Cinderlad was thrown to the floor. Picking himself up he marched outside to see a huge, gleaming horse with the copper armor of a knight on the ground beside it. Cinderlad jumped on the horse and rode it to a hiding place and then went home to his family. For three years in a row Cinderlad kept watch and each year found a horse larger and grander than the last.

Now in this same country there was a king whose daughter he would give to any man who could ride up a mountain of glass and take three golden apples from her lap. The knights came from far and wide, even Cinderlad's brothers came, but no one could ride up the mountain. Finally one last knight rode up to the base of the mountain. He was on a large, grand horse and wore a suit of copper. Who do you suppose he is? And will he win the hand of the princess? To find out read *The Maid on the Glass Mountain.*

About Norway

Norway is a country in Northern Europe, often mentioned as "The Land of the Midnight Sun." For several months of the year the sun shines both night and day in the northern part of the country. Norway is a country of many deep waterways with tall mountains on either side. It has huge glaciers and skiing is a favorite sport. The people of Norway often make their living from the sea as seamen or fishermen. Norway has many small farms. In the cities people live in apartments. Goat cheese is a favorite food since goats adapt better to the mountain life than do cattle.

The Maid on the Glass Mountain

by Peter Asbjornsen

Performing the Booktalk

Speaking Parts: Narrator One, Narrator Two, Cinderlad, Brothers, King

Narrator One: It is midnight on St. John's night and Cinderlad

Cinderlad: is crouched in the hayloft waiting to see what strange creature comes on this special night each year to eat all of the grass in the meadow.

Narrator Two: The two previous years his brothers

Brothers: had been sent to watch, but were so frightened by the clatter and the noise

Narrator Two: that they ran away.

Narrator One: A rumble in the distance grew louder and louder. The hayloft shook and Cinderlad

Cinderlad: was thrown to the floor.

Narrator One: Picking himself up he marched outside

Cinderlad: to see a huge, gleaming horse with the copper armor of a knight on the ground beside it.

Narrator One: Cinderlad jumped on the horse

Cinderlad: and rode it to a hiding place

Narrator One: and then went home to his family. For three years in a row Cinderlad kept watch

Cinderlad: and each year found a horse larger and grander than the last.

The Maid on the Glass Mountain
Performing the Booktalk (continued)

Narrator Two:	Now in this same country there was a king whose daughter he would
King:	give to any man who could ride up a mountain of glass and take three golden apples from her lap.
Narrator Two:	The knights came from far and wide. Even Cinderlad's brothers
Brothers:	came, but no one could ride up the mountain.
Narrator One:	Finally one last knight rode up to the base of the mountain. He was on a large, grand horse and wore a suit of copper.
Narrator Two:	Will *he* win the hand of the princess?
All:	To find out, read, *The Maid on the Glass Mountain.*

Responding to the Booktalk

In small groups discuss the following questions:

1. Who do you believe is the knight in copper armor? Why do you think so?

2. Why do you suppose a story from Norway would feature a large mountain?

3. In what ways are the characters of Cinderlad and Cinderella alike?

The Maid on the Glass Mountain

Recalling the Booktalk in Song

The song below tells about Cinderlad from *The Maid on the Glass Mountain.*

Fill in the blank spaces with the correct word and sing the song to the tune of "My Bonnie Lies Over the Ocean."

hill	ride	noise
Cinderlad	scare	three
grass	hayloft	creatures

Young (1) C ________________ crouched in the (2) h __________
Strange (3) c ___________________________ he waited to see.
A (4) n _________________ in the distance grew louder,
The lad said, "It will not (5) s ________________ me!"

Brothers say he's
The ugliest person in all the land,
Guess who will win
The beautiful maid's lovely hand?

Now (6) t _______________ horses came to the meadow,
Of green (7) g _______________ they had all their fill,
But (8) C __________________ caught them and kept them,
To help him (9) r ____________________ up the glass (10) h ________

Answers: 1. Cinderlad 2. hayloft 3. creatures 4. noise 5. scare 6. three 7. grass 8. Cinderlad 9. ride 10. hill

What Would You Do?

When Cinderlad saw the huge prancing horse eating all of the grass in the field, he knew he had to put a stop to it. He also wanted to capture and keep the horse. But the horse was bigger than any he had ever seen and looked quite fierce. Cinderlad was only a very small boy.

He looked in his backpack and pulled out:

a rope
a rock
a bottle
a blanket
a spoon
a candle
a glass

Work with a partner or small group. Decide how Cinderlad would use any or all of the items in his backpack to capture the horse.

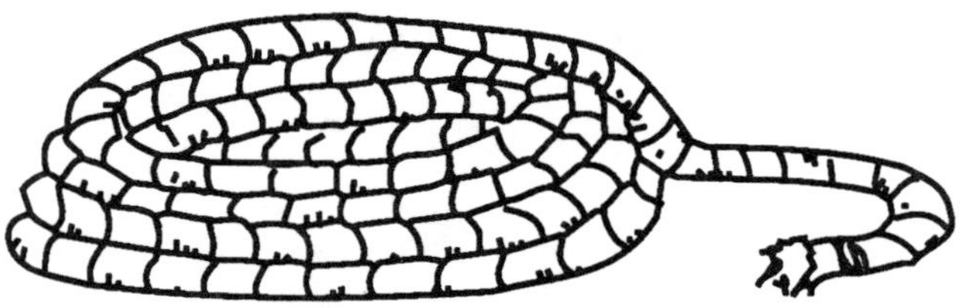

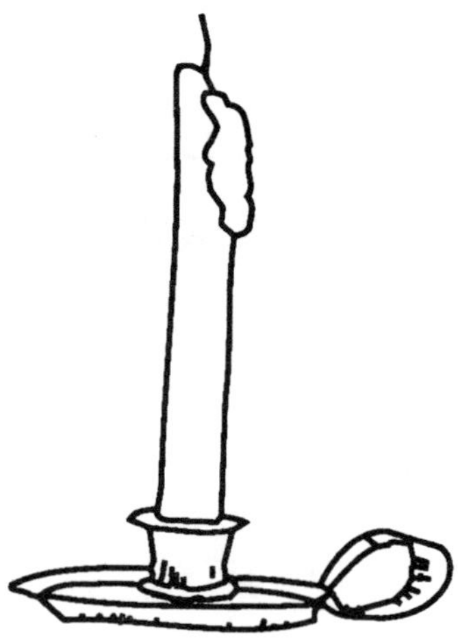

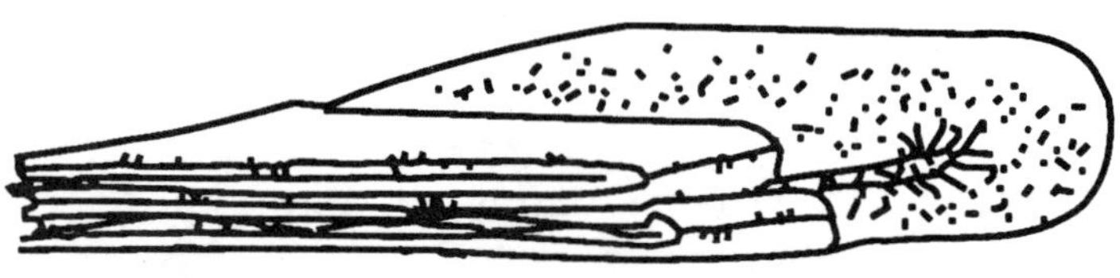

More Picture Story Books About Scandinavia

PICTURE BOOKS

Asbjornsen, Peter Christen. *East of the Sun and West of the Moon*. Illustrated by Kay Nielsen. Doubleday, 1977. (Gr. 3-6)
Six well known tales from Norway.

Galdone, Paul. *The Three Billy Goats Gruff*. Illustrated by the author. Clarion Books, 1973. (Gr. K-3)
Three goats try to cross a bridge without being eaten by the troll.

Greene, Ellin. *The Legend of the Christmas Rose*. Illustrated by Charles Mikolaycak. Holiday House, 1990.
A woman promises to reveal the secret of a miracle to a monk in exchange for getting her husband out of prison.

Hague, Kathleen. *The Man Who Kept House*. Illustrated by Michael Haque. Harcourt, 1981. (Gr. K-3)
A farmer trades places with his wife for the day thinking housework is easier than in the fields.

Haviland, Virginia. *Favorite Fairy Tales Told in Norway*. Illustrated by Leona Weisgaard. Little Brown, 1961.
A collection of easy-to-read tales from Norway.

NON-FICTION

Gascoyne. David. *Norway*. Chelsea, 1984.
Describes the geography, history, people and customs of Norway. A handy reference book for the teacher. Grade six reading level.

St. John, Letty. *A Family in Norway*. Lerner, 1988.
Describes the home, school amusements, customs, work and day-to-day life of ten-year-old Andrea and his family living in a small village just outside Oslo, Norway.

Chancay and the Secret of Fire: A Peruvian Folktale

by Donald Charles. Illustrated by the author.

A Whitebird Book. G. P. Putnam's Sons, 1992

Booktalk

Peru

By sparing the life of the water spirit Tambo, Chancay has proved himself kind and worthy. But to win the secret of fire for his people he must also prove himself strong and brave – braver than anyone has been before.

Over the course of three days, Chancay faces lightning bolts, poisonous spiders, angry panthers, a molten volcano, a terrible condor, and finally, the wrath of the moon and the sun. As Chancay reaches the golden temple where the sun and moon live he knows he must have a clever plan to take the secret of fire home with him for if he fails, the sun will turn him into a shower of sparks and he will be a star forever. What do you suppose Chancay decides to do? Find out in *Chancay and the Secret of Fire.*

About the Author

Donald Charles grew up in the Southwestern United States and as a child attended many Mexican American fiestas and visited Native American trading posts. He often accompanied his brother, a distinguished anthropologist, on field trips and developed a keen interest in folk art and tales from many cultures. He now shares his interest and knowledge in picture books for children about other cultures.

Chancay and the Secret of Fire

by Donald Charles. Illustrated by the author.

A Whitebird Book. G. P. Putnam's Sons, 1992

Performing the Booktalk

Speaking Parts: Narrator One, Narrator Two, Chancay, The Sun

Chancay:	By sparing the life of the Water Spirit Tambo,
Narrator One:	Chancay has proved himself
Chancay:	kind and worthy.
Narrator Two:	But to win the secret of fire for his people he must also prove himself
Chancay:	strong and brave – braver than anyone has been before.
Narrator One:	Over the course of three days Chancay faces
Chancay:	lightning bolts, poisonous spiders, angry panthers, a molten volcano, a terrible condor and finally
Sun:	the wrath of the moon and the sun.
Narrator Two:	As Chancay
Chancay:	reaches the golden temple
Sun:	where the sun and the moon live,
Narrator One:	he knows he must have
Chancay:	a clever plan
Narrator One:	to take the secret of fire home with him, for if he fails, the sun
Sun:	will turn him into a shower of sparks and he will be a star forever.
Narrator Two:	What do you suppose Chancay
Chancay:	decides to do?
Narrator One:	Find out in
Both Narrators:	*Chancay and the Secret of Fire.*

Chancay and the Secret of Fire

Responding to the Booktalk

Chancay was kind and worthy and brave and clever. Using the bio-poem outline below, describe Chancay in other ways.

Compare your completed bio-poem with others in your class. On which points did you agree? Disagree?

Chancay

First name ______________________

Four traits ______________________

Related to ______________________

Cares deeply about ______________________

Who feels ______________________

Who needs ______________________

Who gives ______________________

Who would like to see ______________________

Resident of ______________________

Using this same pattern, write a bio-poem about yourself.

Your name ______________

First name ______________________

Four traits ______________________

Related to ______________________

Cares deeply about ______________________

Who feels ______________________

Who needs ______________________

Who gives ______________________

Who would like to see ______________________

Resident of ______________________

Chancay and the Secret of Fire

Let's Write

Chancay met many creatures that are found in Peru on his journey. He also encountered other dangers in the form of lightning bolts and volcanos. If you followed Chancay's footsteps in traveling through Peru, you would meet these things, too.

Have fun completing the sentences below following this pattern:

A ______________________ is a ______________________
until it ____________________________ and then it becomes
a ____.

Example:
A spider is a spider until it spins a web and then it becomes a web weaver.

1. A lightning bolt is a lightning bolt until it ______________
   ____________________________________ and then it becomes
   a ____.
2. A panther is a panther until it __________________________
   ____________________________________ and then it becomes
   a ____.
3. A volcano is a volcano until it __________________________
   ____________________________________ and then it becomes
   a ____.
4. A sun is the sun until it ____________________________
   ____________________________________ and then it becomes
   a ____.

About Peru

Peru is a country in South America located on the Pacific Coast. It is a land filled with high mountains...the snow-peaked Andes mountains run the entire length of Peru. Most of the people along the coast work on small farms or large plantations. The mountain people herd cattle, llamas or sheep. The llama is especially suited to mountain life and many are found in Peru. The people use the llama for transportation and carrying goods. The llama hair is used to make clothing, while the hide is used for sandals. The Indians of Peru eat the meat of the young llama.
Find out about the llama. Add one or two additional facts to each list below.

Data Bank - Llama

Lives	**Eats**	**What It Has**
Peru	shrubs	thick, long hair
______	____________	________________________
______	____________	________________________
______	____________	________________________

What it Does	**Looks Like**
carries loads	five feet tall
travels 20 miles a day	brown, buff, gray, white or black
____________________	____________________________
____________________	____________________________
____________________	____________________________

Use the information in your data bank to write a song about the llama. (Tune: London Bridge)

A llama has nice thick long hair
Thick long hair
Thick long hair
A llama has nice thick long hair
And is five feet tall.

A llama carries ___________________________
____
____
A llama carries ___________________________
And ______________________________________

Write a Fact or Fiction Book about Volcanos

On the fourth day of his travels Chancay came upon a smoldering crater and in the center of the crater were molten red rocks.

Read about volcanoes in the encyclopedia or in a book about volcanoes. Two good books are: *Volcano* by Lionel Bender. Watts, 1988. (Gr. 3-4). *Volcano* by Patricia Lauer. Bradbury, 1986. (Gr. 4-6)

Fact or Fiction Book

Fact or Fiction?

Lava from a volcano is heated by the sun.

Fiction

Lava from a volcano is molten rock from cracks deep within the earth.

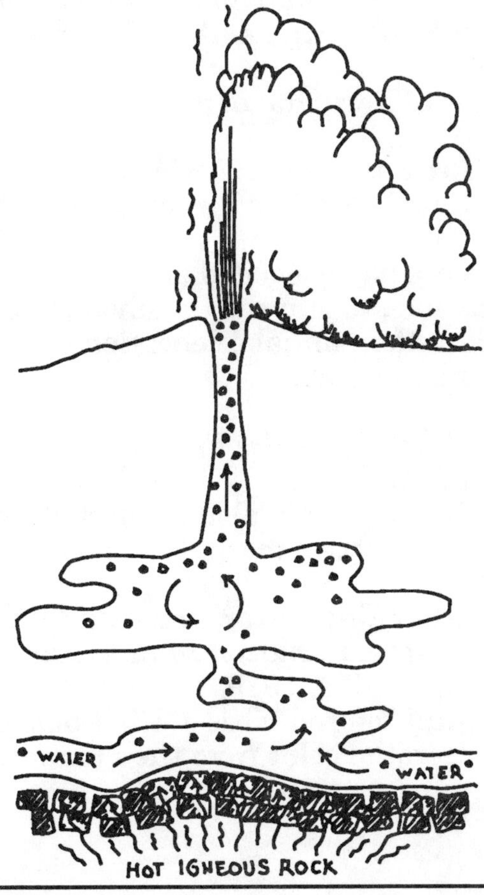

Example:

1. Make a statement about the topic on one page and ask your reader to guess if the statement is fact or fiction.

2. On the next page, tell if the statement is fact or fiction and why. Illustrate the pages.

More Tales from South America

PICTURE BOOKS

Alexander, Ellen. *Llama and the Great Flood: A Folktale From Peru.* Illustrated by the author. Crowell, 1989.
A llama warns his master of a coming great flood.

Carlson, Lori M. and Cynthia L. Ventura, Editors. *Where Angels Glide: New Stories From Latin America.* Illustrated by Jose Ortega. HarperCollins 1990. Intermediate Grades.
Ten short stories from Central America, South America and the Caribbean.

Dewey, Arianne. *The Thunder God's Son.* Illustrated by the author. Greenwillow, 1981.
A tale of Peru and of magic.

Dorros, Arthur. *Tonight is Carnival.* Illustrated by Club de Madres Virgen del Carmen. Dutton, 1991.
A young boy is excited as he gets, for the first time, to join the Carnival band to take part in the annual celebration in a Peruvian village.

Finger, Charles J. *Tales From Silver Lands.* Doubleday, 1924.
Stories to be read aloud collected from all parts of South America.

Flora. Author-Illustrator. *Feathers Like a Rainbow: An Amazon Indian Tale.* HarperCollins, 1989.
The dull colored birds of the Amazon steal the secret of color from the hummingbird.

NON-FICTION

Cobbs, Vicki. *This Place is High.* Illustrated by Barbara Lauallee. Walker, 1989. (Gr. 2-3)
Carries children to the top of the Andes Mountains in Bolivia and Peru to describe life in a very high place, including the exotic animals found there.

Morrison, Marion. *Indians of the Andes.* Rourke Pubs., 1987. (Gr. 4-6)
Introduces the history, culture, and daily life of the Indians who live in the highlands of South America's Andes Mountains.

Peru in Pictures. Prepared by the Geography Department. Lerner Publications, 1987. (Gr. 4-6)
Photographs and brief text introduce the geography, history, people and culture of Peru.

St. John, Letty. *A Family in Peru.* Photos by Nigel Harvey. Lerner, 1987.
Describes the home, customs, work, and amusements of a Peruvian girl and her family who live in the Andes Mountains.

Salt

from a collection of Russian folktales by Alexander Afanasiev

Illustrated picture book versions include:

Salt retold by Jane Langton. Illustrated by Isle Plume. Hyperion Books, 1992

Salt retold by Harve Zemach. Illustrated by Margot Zemach. Follett, 1965

Booktalk

Russia

A merchant father sends his three sons in cargo-laden ships to make their fortunes. The two older sons lose their cargos but the youngest son, Ivan, finds an island with a mountain of salt and trades the salt to the Tsar for gold, silver jewels and the Tsar's daughter. On the return journey Ivan sees his brothers' battered ships and takes them aboard his ship. The jealous brothers toss Ivan overboard and make their way home with the Tsar's daughter who weeps all the way. With the help of a giant, Ivan arrives home just in time to put things straight and to marry the Tsar's daughter... proving that he is not so much as a fool as everyone thought.

About the Collector and the Country

Alexander Afanasiev was a well known Russian writer who collected many of the most popular Russian folktales and preserved them in several collections. From these collections many of the tales have been retold and illustrated as beautiful picture books. At the time the tales were collected, Russia was one part of the former Soviet Union, a land that stretched from the Baltic Sea in the West to the Pacific Ocean in the East and from the frozen Arctic in the North to hot deserts in the South. The land is so vast that the day begins in the East eleven hours before it reaches the West. In 1991 the Soviet Union was dissolved and became a number of independent nations, one of these being Russia.

Salt

by Alexander Afanasiev

Performing the Booktalk

Speaking Parts: Narrator One, Narrator Two, Ivan, Two Brothers

Narrator One:	A merchant-father sends his three sons
Narrator Two:	in cargo-laden ships to make their fortunes. The two older sons lose their cargos
Narrator One:	but the youngest son, Ivan,
Ivan:	finds an island with a mountain of salt and trades the salt to the Tsar for gold, silver, jewels and the Tsar's daughter.
Narrator One:	On the return journey Ivan see his brothers'
Ivan:	battered ships and takes them aboard
Narrator Two:	his ship. The jealous brothers
Brothers:	toss Ivan overboard
Narrator Two:	and make their way home
Brothers:	with the Tsar's daughter who weeps all the way.
Narrator One:	With the help of a giant, Ivan
Ivan:	arrives home just in time to put things straight,
Narrator Two:	and to marry the Tsar's daughter,
Narrator One:	proving that he is not
Ivan:	so much of a fool
Narrators & Brothers:	as everyone thought!

Salt
Recalling the Story in Song

Choose words that best fit the blank spaces. Then sing the song to the tune of "My Bonnie Lies Over the Ocean."

Ivan	round	salt	giant	fool
father	overboard	pocket	Earth	ship
gold	home	school	Tsar	silver
kopecks	island			

Young (1) I ________________ sailed over the ocean
Most people thought he was a (2) f ________________
But while at sea (3) I ______________ would learn more,
Than if he were going to (4) s ____________________ .

Chorus
Ivan questioned
The shape of the (5) E ______________
Was is flat or (6) r ________________
(7) F ____________________ answered
"It's flat, son, just look at the ground.

His (8) s ______________ sailed up to a small (9) i ______________
Topped off with a big salty hill,
For this the great (10) T ____________ would pay (11) k __________
His silver salt shakers to fill.

The boy traded (12) s ______________ for some treasures,
His brothers threw him (13) o ____________________ ,
Then counted the (14) g ______________ and the (15) s __________ ,
A truly magnificent hoard.

But Ivan is saved by a (16) g ________________
Who over the (17) E ______________ likes to roam,
He puts the brave boy in his (18) p __________________
And carries him all the way (19) h __________________________

Answers: 1. Ivan 2. fool 3. Ivan 4. school 5. Earth 6. round 7. Father 8. ship 9. island 10. Tsar 11. kopecks 12. salt 13. overboard 14. gold 15. silver 16. giant 17. Earth 18. pocket 19. home

"If I Were" Pattern

In the story, *Salt*, Ivan needed many things to help him win the hand of the tsarevna. He needed a sailing ship to take him across the ocean. He used the salt to flavor the food so the tsarevna would eat. He needed the giant to get him back home.

Use the pattern below to tell how each of these things helped Ivan.

"If I Were" Pattern

1. Name the thing you want to be
2. Where is it found?
3. One thing it would do for someone else
4. A second thing it would do
5. Repeat the first line

If I were a ______________________

On (or in) ______________________

I would ______________________

And ______________________

If I were a ______________________

Example:

If I were a shaker of salt
Sitting in your kitchen
I would get the tsarevna to eat more
By flavoring her soup
If I were a shaker of salt.

If I were a sailing ship
On (or in) ______________________
I would ______________________
And ______________________
If I were a ______________________

If I were a giant
On (or in) ______________________
I would ______________________
And ______________________
If I were a ______________________

About Russia

Today Russia is an independent nation but was until recently a republic in the Soviet Union. Many years ago all of the land was ruled by a king called a Tsar. Most of the royal families lived in St. Petersburg which is today called Leningrad. In Moscow, the largest city in Russia, families live in apartments. There are very few private homes. Russian children go to school for ten years. A kopeck is a Russian coin. Until Glasnost, or the time of openness, the people of Russia did not have a great deal of freedom but this is rapidly changing. At the time of the Tsars the land they ruled was so vast that when people in Moscow were going to bed, those in Vladivostock were having breakfast!

To learn more about Russia, choose a project from the chart that follows. Choose a topic, choose a verb and choose a product.

Verb	Topic	Product
List	common animals found in Russia	Fact/Fiction Book
Describe	Life in Moscow today	Poem
Summarize	Going to school in Russia	Drawing
Compare		Song
		Report

Sample Statements:

I will list common animals found in Russia in a drawing.

I will describe life today in Moscow in a Fact/Fiction book.

I will summarize going to school in Russia in a song.

Fact or Fiction Books

Fact or Fiction?

For hundreds of years Russia was called "the sleeping bear of the world."

Fact

Long after other countries had modern factories, the people of Russia were still farmers, using the same hand tools their ancestors used to till the land. There were no modern factories until the 1900s.

Make your own fact or fiction book about Russia.

1. On one page you make a statement about Russia and ask your reader if the statement is fact or fiction.

2. On the next page you tell your reader whether the statement is fact or fiction and why.

3. Your book can have as many pages as you wish.

More Tales from Russia

PICTURE BOOKS

Afanasyev, Alexander. *The Fool and the Fish*. Illustrated by Gennady Spirin. Dial, 1990.
A lazy fool catches an enchanted fish which promises him that every wish he makes will come true.

Dalgliesh, Alice and Milhous, Katherine. *The Turnip*. Illustrated by Pierr Morgan. Coward-McCann, 1983.
A turnip grows so big that the whole family has to pull it up.

Ginsburg, Mirra. *The Magic Stove*. Illustrated by Linda Heller. Coward-McCann, 1983.
An old man, his wife and their rooster enjoy wonderful pies made by their magic stove until a greedy king arrives.

Lemieux, Michele. *Peter and the Wolf*. Illustrated by the author. Morrow, 1991.
A small boy uses his wits to defeat a wolf in the meadow.

Ransome, Arthur. *The Fool of the World and the Flying Ship*. Illustrated by Uri Shulevitz. Farrar, Straus and Giroux, 1968.
The fool of the world sets out to find a flying ship for the Czar and picks up peasants who will help him in his quest to marry the Czar's daughter.

Small, Ernest. *Baba Yaga*. Illustrated by Blair Lent. Houghton Mifflin, 1966.
A small girl is captured by a witch and helps Baba Yaga to find a magical flower.

Tompert, Ann. *The Tzar's Bird*. Illustrated by Robert Rayevsky. Macmillan, 1990.
A witch presents a prince with a firebird warning him that if anything should happen to the bird the prince will be doomed.

Winthrop, Elizabeth (adapted by) *Vasilissa The Beautiful: A Russian Folktale*. Illustrated by Alexander Koshkin. HarperCollins, 1991.
Poor Vasilissa with her magic doll overcomes many trials from her stepmother, stepsisters and the evil witch, Baba Yaga.

Wolkstein, Diane. *Oom Razoom Or Go I Know Not Where, Bring Back I Know Not What*. Illustrated by Dennis McDermott. Morrow, 1992.
A king sends a huntsman on an endless voyage with a surprise waiting at the journey's end.

Subject Index